C0-AVA-439

THE FORM AND POWER OF RELIGION

The Form and Power of Religion

John Wesley on Methodist Vitality

Laura Bartels Felleman

CASCADE *Books* • Eugene, Oregon

THE FORM AND POWER OF RELIGION
John Wesley on Methodist Vitality

Cascade Books
An Imprint of Wipf and Stock Publishers
199 W. 8th Ave., Suite 3
Eugene, OR 97401

www.wipfandstock.com

ISBN 13: 978-1-61097-778-4

Cataloging-in-Publication data:

Felleman, Laura Bartels.

The form and power of religion : John Wesley on Methodist vitality / Laura Bartels Felleman.

xii + 106 p. ; 23 cm. —Includes bibliographical references and index.

ISBN 13: 978-1-61097-778-4

1. Wesley, John, 1703–1791. 2. Methodism—History. I. Title.

BX8331.3 .F35 2012

Manufactured in the U.S.A.

Contents

Preface

You are a minister—a Christ-centered, Spirit-filled, called-of-God minister. By virtue of your baptism you are responsible for the ministry of the church as preacher, teacher, motivator, consoler, advocate, or counselor. To prepare for this vocation you gain firsthand experience, attend workshops, read books, take classes, confide in mentors, and pray without ceasing.

You till soil, sow seeds, eliminate weeds, and then look for spiritual fruits, knowing that neither annual nor perennial returns may sprout from your efforts. The seeds you plant could lie dormant for decades or mature underground, out of sight and undetected, but causing real growth nonetheless.

Some determine the impact of their ministry by figuring census counts and tallying donations, but for you equating progress in ministry with numerical increases feels too worldly. Your religious sensibilities are offended by the idea. Instead, you desire a qualitative measurement of the effect your ministry has had on others.

Regrettably, discerning maturation in faith, perceiving an increase in love, and assessing the health of a soul are subjective judgments, and you know that disguising subjectivity in the form of objective reporting is unethical. If esoteric growth is unquantifiable, you are left with no other choice but to supply the statistics that can be computed. When your supervisor requests an end-of-year report, you will comply and fill in the forms. Data on attendance, offerings, baptisms, professions of faith, transfers of membership, and numbers served will be compiled. You will send the denomination what it requires so that it can generate the charts and figures that it uses to determine the state of the church.

Unhappily for you, this means that your professional reason for being—the privilege of helping others grow spiritually—is not recounted in your yearly ministry overview.

Evidence-based evaluations are required in a number of professions. Teachers and therapists as well as clergy are now asked to prove how well they are performing on the job. When business and science professionals evaluate their work, they typically defend it by diagramming their quarterly profits or publishing their latest discoveries. Professionals within the humanities cannot offer comparable results to corroborate their claims of competency, and yet they must nonetheless somehow prove their efficacy.

In The United Methodist Church, ordained elders must substantiate their professional integrity by undergoing an annual review of their ministry. The origin of this effectiveness protocol was a petition jointly submitted to the 2008 General Conference by the Council of Bishops, The General Board of Discipleship, and The General Board of Higher Education and Ministry. After debate and revision, the members of the Ministry and Higher Education legislative committee voted seventy-two in favor, one against, and one abstaining to adopt the petition as amended. The petition was then placed on a consent calendar with eighty-three other petitions and approved *en masse* by the General Conference plenary session on April 30.[1]

This legislative action expanded a paragraph in The United Methodist *Book of Discipline* on the "Ministry, Authority, and Responsibilities of an Elder in Full Connection" (¶334). Included in this expansion was a procedure for addressing the ineffectiveness of an elder. The procedure stipulates that whenever concerns are raised about an elder, the bishop must respond by designing a plan of action that will help the elder rectify any professional inadequacies. Even with this intervention, the expectations of success are low and the disciplinary paragraph ends pessimistically: "Upon evaluation, determine that the plan of action has not been carried out or produced fruit that gives a realistic expectation of future effectiveness" (¶334.3c).

The 2012 General Conference adopted new guidelines for bishops to follow once an elder has been judged to be hopelessly ineffective. The General Board of Higher Education and Ministry proposed and the General Conference delegates approved a new paragraph in the *Book of Discipline* that sets out the steps that must be taken by the bishop, the Board of

1. Greenwaldt, Lyght, and Del Pino, "Petition 80251—Guaranteed Appointments."

Ordained Ministry, and the clergy session of annual conference in order to "fire" an ineffective elder.[2]

Ministerial effectiveness is intentionally left undefined in ¶334. Through its Board of Ordained Ministry and cabinet, each annual conference is to establish its own standard for judging the "vocational competence" of elders (¶334.4). Recognizing that conference leaders would be searching for guidance as they implemented this policy, I began researching the possibility of using John Wesley as a defining example of clergy effectiveness.

My original intention was to write a book that accounted for the tremendous impact that Wesley's ministry had on others. Given his success as an ordained elder, as well as the fact that every pastor of Wesleyan and Methodist churches is an inheritor of his legacy, I reasoned that a study of Wesley's effectiveness as the leader of a vital Christian ministry would give pastors an inspiring role model to emulate as they strove to meet the expectations of their denominational leaders.

In the years before and after the 2008 General Conference, the United Methodist bishops seemed particularly receptive to the notion that Wesley's ecclesiastical descendants should still be patterning themselves after the example of their founder. The Council of Bishops made the church's Wesleyan identity the focus of the 2007 Convocation for Extended Cabinets, an international event that was attended by almost nine hundred United Methodist bishops, district superintendents, and other cabinet members.[3]

At the convocation, Dr. Randy Maddox, Professor of Theology and Wesleyan Studies at Duke Divinity School, presented a paper that summarized Wesley's model for ministry and argued that the church had become spiritually lethargic because it had abandoned Wesleyan principles. The paper, "Living the United Methodist Way," then set forth a plan for denominational renewal by recovering the "Crucial Dynamics of the Methodist Way: Doctrine, Spirit, and Discipline."[4]

The slogan "Living the United Methodist Way" began to appear on UM-related websites and blogs soon after the convocation ended. Many of those who attended the event expressed their appreciation for the gathering, as well as their hope that returning to Wesleyan practices would lead to the revitalization of churches.[5]

2. Cape, "Petition 20173— Complaint Process Revision: Administrative Location."

3. Green, "Convocation Focuses on 'The United Methodist Way.'"

4. "The United Methodist Way."

5. Coyner, "857 Plus One"; Burton-Edwards, "Commentary"; Haller, "Commentary"; and Whitaker, "Living the United Methodist Way."

The idea of recapturing Wesley and thus "Living the United Methodist Way" was shared with the wider denomination through a variety of venues. Dr. Maddox, in plenary addresses to the 2008 Florida Annual Conference and the 2008 Southeastern Jurisdictional Conference, expanded on his earlier presentation and further explained Methodism's original Doctrine, Spirit, and Discipline. The 2009 United Methodist quadrennial training event for more than twelve hundred annual conference leaders also focused on "Living the United Methodist Way."[6] In addition, the 2010 Laity Convocation of the Arkansas Annual Conference was advertised as an opportunity to dialogue about "the United Methodist Way, regaining the passion of our founders, reconnecting with our Wesleyan core values, reawakening our hearts for ministry with the poor, and the revitalization of the United Methodist Church in Arkansas."[7]

As a United Methodist elder and a John Wesley scholar, I felt compelled to join the effort to rediscover the reasons for Wesley's effectiveness as a religious leader. The longer I worked on that project, however, the clearer it became that I needed to write to a broader audience. I came to realize that Wesley's example had relevance for every church member, not solely the elders, because his vision for Methodist vitality depended on more than effective clergy; it required the effective participation of the entire organization, both the laity and the clergy.

My interest in John Wesley was first piqued by Dr. Dale Dunlap in his United Methodist History course at Saint Paul School of Theology. As Dr. Dunlap read segments of Wesley's *Journal* to the class, I remember thinking how fortunate the Methodists were to have all these first-person accounts of the early years of the movement.

Ten years later I began a closer reading of those primary sources as part of my Doctor of Ministry research. Dr. Henry Knight added to my understanding of Wesley, and I was fortunate to receive his direction as I explored the implications of Wesley's doctrine of Christian Perfection for the United Methodist Order of Elders.

Working on the DMin heightened my motivation to study Wesley and, after discerning that I was supposed to continue my research, I enrolled in the Wesleyan and Methodist Studies PhD program at Drew University as an answer to that call. I was blessed to make the acquaintance of Dr.

6. Maddox, "Living the United Methodist Way"; and Pinkston and Alsgaard, "United Methodists Join Forces."

7. Village United Methodist Church, "Upcoming Events," *The Chimes*.

Maddox during that time, and I appreciate his continuing mentorship. Dr. Richard Heitzenrater has also been a source of inspiration and encouragement as I continue to learn historical research methods and apply them to Wesley's texts.

My postdoctoral research could not have been accomplished without the aid of Mark Shenise at the United Methodist Archives and the help of the library staff at Memphis Theological Seminary. I am indebted to them for all the materials they acquired for me.

At times I questioned whether I would ever find a way to organize these materials around a coherent theme. Prayer helped. The support of my family did, too. My husband, Dirk, is especially deserving of acknowledgment for putting up with the "bad writing days," which always seemed to outnumber the good. He knew the truth—this too shall pass—and I am grateful for his wisdom.

Finally, after years of reading, ruminating, and rewriting, a phrase jumped out at me: "having the form of religion without the power." I had read this passage in Wesley's article "Thoughts upon Methodism" many times without taking any particular notice of it. This time the words sparked my curiosity, and the shape of my thesis began to emerge as I tried to understand what Wesley meant by this statement and to think through what its implications were for the Wesleyans of today. To those working on their own writing projects I offer this advice—keep mulling over the form of your research while awaiting the power that gives insight. It will come.

> Now to the one who by the power at work within us is able to accomplish abundantly far more than all we can ask or imagine, to God be glory in the church and in Christ Jesus to all generations, forever and ever. Amen. (Eph 3:20–21)

Abbreviations

AM	*Arminian Magazine*. Edited by John Wesley. London, 1778–1791. British Periodicals Database http://search.proquest.com./britishperiodicals
Letters	*The Letters of John Wesley*. Edited by John Telford. Wesley Center Online Version http://wesley.nnu.edu/john-wesley/the-letters-of-john-wesley/
Library	*A Christian Library*. Edited by John Wesley. Bristol: Felix Farley, 1749–1755.
Notes	John Wesley, *Explanatory Notes upon the New Testament*. Wesley Center Online Version http://wesley.nnu.edu/john-wesley/john-wesleys-notes-on-the-bible/
SOSO	John Wesley, *Sermons on Several Occasions*. Vol. 4. Bristol: John Grabham, 1760.
Works	*The Works of John Wesley: The Bicentennial Edition*. General editors, Frank Baker and Richard P. Heitzenrater. Nashville: Abingdon, 1976–.
Works (Jackson)	*The Works of John Wesley*. Edited by Thomas Jackson. 3rd ed. 1872. Reprint. Grand Rapids: Baker, 2002.

ONE

Advising Christian Readers

I am not afraid that the people called Methodists should ever cease to exist either in Europe or America. But I am afraid, lest they should only exist as a dead sect, having the form of religion without the power. And this undoubtedly will be the case, unless they hold fast both the doctrine, spirit, and discipline with which they first set out.

—*Thoughts upon Methodism*

DISCERNING THE OUTWARD FORMS of religion is a simple matter of perception. We see the rituals, hear the liturgies and songs, smell the incense, feel the weight of sacred texts, and taste the foods laden with symbolic meaning. Religious practices are knowable in a physical sense even when their spiritual significance escapes our understanding.

The same cannot be said of the power of religion. This dimension of religion is undetectable by the five senses. We may know religious practitioners whose personalities have suddenly changed for the better (she is more loving, he is more joyful, they are more charitable and less materialistic), but observing these changes is not the same as discerning the power that caused the transformation.

We have no objective way to verify that they are telling the truth, that they are not deceiving us or themselves, when the devout claim that they have experienced the power to which the form of religion points. We have no means of assessing the kind of force that has been exerted on them, or of measuring the impression left by its impact, or of gauging the fluctuations in the power's influence over them. Such things can be captured neither by our physical senses nor by our research instruments.

The undetectability of the power of religion creates a dilemma for those using scientific methods to investigate the practice of ministry. The authors of the 2007 study of clergy effectiveness commissioned by the General Board of Higher Education and Ministry of The United Methodist Church faced just such a research quandary. In their report the researchers admit that their analysis focuses only on "the observable behaviors and tasks performed in the job of a local pastor and is likely incapable of adequately capturing important but unobservable states such as being in a state of worship, prayer, or grace."

While recognizing that pastoral effectiveness is typically equated with a pastor's ability to have a spiritual influence on parishioners, to boldly lead them and evoke within them "a genuine desire for spiritual growth" so that they are transformed and "become better, more spiritual people who make better decisions and have stronger, healthier relationships with God and others," the researchers are unable to explain how pastors achieve this goal.

Consequently, the report merely lists the tasks commonly performed by pastors but can not explain how these outward tasks contribute to the ability to effectively influence the inward spiritual lives of parishioners. Confessing that "the relative importance of these task clusters is not known," the researchers confide that they will need to conduct more studies before they can advise the General Board on how best to train effective pastors.[1]

The Apostle Paul was less tentative when giving his advice to church leaders. He knew who had the power of religion and who did not. He knew what it was, what was conducive to it, and what was obstructive. Moreover, he knew how to influence others spiritually so that they could experience this transforming power for themselves.

He was certain, for example, that Timothy had experienced the power of religion, "a spirit of power and of love and of self-discipline." Paul associated this power with the grace of God given to those who had faith in Christ. Timothy, as a next-generation Christian leader, was advised to put this power into practice (2 Tim 1:7–9).

As the pastoral leader of the church in Ephesus, Timothy was instructed to oversee the church's public forms of religion (e.g., corporate prayers, the reading of Scripture, and charitable works).[2] In order to effectively

1. DeShon and Quinn, *Job Analysis Generalizability Study*, 8–20.

2. 1 Tim 2:1, 8, 10; 4:13–16; 6:18–19; 2 Tim 3:16.

carry out this ministry, Timothy was to practice private forms of religion that would train him in godliness (inward religious convictions expressed through outward pious behaviors). Paul's training regimen for ministers required Timothy to shun youthful passions, be virtuous, keep the commandments, be respectful when talking to others, and avoid those who had the form of godliness but denied the power that was the source of true religion.[3]

Over the centuries, other church leaders wrote about their experience of the power of religion and advised Christians on how they could experience God's grace for themselves. Unfortunately, these early Christian writings were expensive and scarce prior to the print revolution. Hand-copied by monastic scribes and decorated with miniature paintings, these illuminated books were in the possession of the church and the wealthy but not the majority of Christians.

Only after the invention of movable type were books of religious instruction made available to a wider audience. Once the presses began production, a market for Bibles, catechisms, and devotional literature emerged in every Protestant country, and trade routes were established that transported books over continents and across oceans.[4] This new industry allowed Christians to supplement the ministry of their parish priest with spiritual advice from beyond the borders of their neighborhood, nation, and era.

In cities throughout Germany, England, and the Netherlands, a new Christian community formed. In these religious societies, lay readers of religious advice books supported and encouraged one another as they each tried to follow the instructions that would keep their faith vital and full of the power of God's grace.[5]

John Wesley was one such reader. He began reading religious advice books while he was a graduate student at Oxford University. At first, he discussed these books with his parents in letters he exchanged with them. Eventually, a small group formed around him at the University, and together John, his brother Charles, and a few friends studied the bestsellers in practical divinity and encouraged one another in their efforts to experience the power of religion.

3. 1 Tim 4:7; 5:1–2; 6:11–16; 2 Tim 2:22, 25; 3:1–5. For Paul's definition of godliness see Towner, *The Letters to Timothy and Titus*, 171–74.

4. Eisenstein, *The Printing Press as an Agent of Change*, 346.

5. Davies, "Introduction," in *Works* 9:6; Kisker, "Anthony Horneck," 114–15.

Before long John became the author of religious advice books in his own right, and his publishing career provided thousands of inexpensive religious texts to the Methodists—members of religious societies in Britain and America who looked to Wesley as their spiritual guide.

Wesley's religious advice to the Methodists is similar to that found in Paul's letters to Timothy. Wesley also identified who had experienced the power of religion, what it was, what fostered it, what obstructed it, and how to help others experience it. Also like Paul, Wesley encouraged the Methodists to beware of those who had the form of godliness but denied its power.

Wesley criticized the tendency to reduce Christian discipleship to "harmlessness, using the means of grace, and doing good," a standard that he associated with the form of godliness without the power.[6] Church members who lived by this lesser standard did have a kind of faith, Wesley conceded. Harmless people could be so blameless that they shunned everything contrary to God's moral law as set forth in the Ten Commandments and the Gospels. Those who obeyed God's standard of morality did not swear, they observed the Sabbath, they avoided morally questionable situations and behaviors, they would not retaliate when wronged, and their conduct was consistently guided by the rule, Do not do unto others what you would not want done unto you. They were good people who sincerely attempted to serve God and willingly tried to promote the physical and spiritual well-being of others through acts of charity. Their own faith was supported by their regular participation in Means of Grace such as public, family, and private prayers, participation in the Lord's Supper, fasting, as well as hearing and reading Scripture.[7]

Nevertheless, for as much as Wesley admired the form of godliness, it only amounted to the performance of outward rites and duties and thus lacked the "vital inward principle" of religion. For Wesley, genuine discipleship occurred when external righteousness sprang from a power that produced internal righteousness.[8]

Wesley's description of the nature of this power is based on a salvation history commonly recounted in the religious advice books he read. The

6. Sermon 2, "The Almost Christian," I.4–13, and Journal entry, 25 May 1739, *Works* 1:132–37; 19:123–24.

7. Sermon 7, I.4–5, Sermon 22, II.4, Sermon 25, "Sermon on the Mount, V," IV.7–8, and Sermon 33, I.1–3, *Works* 1:219–20, 496–97, 565–67, 688–89.

8. Sermon 29, "Sermon on the Mount, IX," §22, Sermon 45, "The New Birth," III.1, Sermon 62, "The End of Christ's Coming," III.5; and Wesley to Richard Morgan, Sen., 15 March 1734, *Works* 1:644, 2:194, 482–83; 25:381.

history begins with the Genesis account of the creation of humanity in the image of God and describes how the *imago Dei* was damaged by the Fall. Because of the predicament of the fallen *imago Dei*, an interior renovation is necessary, something that exterior religion cannot accomplish.[9]

Only grace can renew the image of God. Wesley defined grace as both the unmerited mercy offered to sinners who believe in Christ, and as the power of God at work within believers through the operation of the Holy Spirit. By grace and through faith, the *imago Dei* is healed, and Christians are enabled to imitate Christ and pattern their thoughts, words, and actions after his example. Just as Paul had encouraged his readers, so too Wesley encouraged the Methodists to press on towards this prize—the complete renewal of the *imago Dei* in true righteousness and holiness (Eph 4:24).

Practicing the form of godliness while waiting for the power of godliness was the only way to renew the image of God, Wesley advised the Methodists, and he expected them to support one another as they practiced and waited. The form of godliness (i.e., do no harm, do good, use all the ordinances of God) was a minimum membership requirement for Wesley's religious societies, and the Methodists were instructed to hold one another accountable to that standard. They were to practice outward forms of religion (including ceasing harmful behaviors, increasing helpful activities, participating in devotional exercises, engaging in holy conversations, and denying the self by submitting to God's will) while waiting for the inward experience of grace received through faith.[10]

Wesley was well aware of other religious movements that had at first enjoyed vigorous starts similar to the one his Methodists were undergoing only to eventually forsake the power, inevitably settle into the form, and finally lose even the outward appearance of religiosity. Yet despite this pervasive pattern, Wesley assured his followers that this did not have to be the fate of Methodism. If they followed his advice and simultaneously held on to the outer form and the inner power of religion, then the Methodists would remain a vital faith community. In his article "Thoughts upon Methodism," Wesley identified the components of an effective ministry design that would help readers follow his instructions and become mature Christians.

9. Sermon 44, "Original Sin," *Works* 2:172–85.

10. Sermon 85, "On Working Out Our Own Salvation," II.4, *Works* 3:205–6.

A Founder's Final Thoughts

The possibility that Methodism in Europe or America would lose its vitality and die out seemed unlikely when John Wesley penned these thoughts in 1786. At that point the Methodist renewal movement within the Church of England had been underway for almost fifty years. Every major industrial center in the British Isles contained Methodist societies. American Methodists, with Wesley's approval, had just organized into an independent denomination. Methodism in the decade of the eighties was experiencing another wave of revival.

At the 1780 session of the Methodist Conference the membership totals reported for Europe and America were 43,830 and 10,139, respectively.[11] Within six years those figures had increased by 33 percent in Europe and had more than doubled in America.[12] Testimonials from revivals occurring all over the British Isles, including the circuits of Thurlton, Huddiscom, London, Bristol, Manchester, Ashton, Oldham, Epworth, and Cornwall, were circulated in Wesley's *Arminian Magazine* and in his *Journals*.[13] Meanwhile, in America, the journal entries of Francis Asbury for this same time period note signs of Methodist progress in New York, Pennsylvania, Virginia, Maryland, New Jersey, and Delaware.[14]

These indications of Methodist vitality stood in stark contrast to the signs of Wesley's physical decline. The founder of Methodism no longer traveled the circuits on horseback; his eyesight was weakening, his stamina was beginning to wane, and he experienced more memory lapses. Twice in 1783 he was seriously ill, first during his annual meeting with the Methodist preachers and then again a few months later.[15]

In 1784 Wesley began the process of transferring his authority to the next generation of Methodist leaders. In February of that year, heeding the encouragement of the lawyer-preacher Thomas Coke and the attendees of the 1783 Conference, Wesley registered a deed for Methodist properties, which stated that the preaching houses were to be held in trust for the one hundred preachers who would constitute the Methodist Conference in the

11. Rack, *Reasonable Enthusiast*, 491.

12. Annual *Minutes* (1786), Q. 11, *Works* 10:612.

13. Rack, *Reasonable Enthusiast*, 492–94, 641; Heitzenrater, *Wesley and the People Called Methodists*, 276–77.

14. Asbury, *The Heart of Asbury's Journal*, 193–239.

15. Rack, *Reasonable Enthusiast*, 528–29; and Journal entries for 5–23 August and 11 October 1783, *Works* 23:287, 291, n 37.

event of his death. In addition, the Deed of Declaration also established the organizational structure and powers of the conference.[16]

Seven months later he ordained three ministers (including the above-mentioned Coke, who was given authority as an episcopal superintendent) for the expanding work in America. Wesley sent the new Methodist priests to America with two books (a revision of Anglican doctrine and liturgy edited by Wesley and a new version of the Methodist hymnal) and a letter endorsing the creation of an independent church.[17]

The Deed of Declaration and the ordinations for America, coupled with the 1785 ordination of three preachers serving Methodist societies in Scotland, fueled speculation that Wesley was preparing to leave the Church of England and establish his own denomination.[18]

Even Charles seemed unsure of his brother's intentions during this period. He wrote to John soon after the Scotland ordinations and pleaded with him to prayerfully reread the 1758 Methodist tract "Reason against a Separation" (especially Hymn Seven) and to refrain from engaging in actions that would bring shame on the family name.[19]

To quell the mounting rumors, Wesley published a series of pro-Church, anti-schism position statements in the *Arminian Magazine*. First, he went public with the reply he had written in response to the letter from Charles. He was as staunchly against leaving the church as ever, he assured his brother (and his readers): "I still attend all the ordinances of the Church, at all opportunities. And I constantly and earnestly advise all that are connected with me so to do."[20]

16. Rack, *Reasonable Enthusiast*, 502–5; Heitzenrater, *Wesley*, 282–85.

17. Rack, *Reasonable Enthusiast*, 513; Heitzenrater, *Wesley*, 287–90.

18. Rack, *Reasonable Enthusiast*, 519; Heitzenrater, *Wesley*, 294.

19. Jackson, *Charles Wesley*, 2:728–29. The third stanza of Hymn Seven predicts that

> Soon as their guides are taken home
> We know the grievous wolves will come,
> Determined not to spare;
> The stragglers from thy wounded side
> The wolves will into sects divide,
> And into parties tear. *Works*: 9:348, lines 15–20

Near the end of 1785, Charles wrote a tract that was critical of Coke and anonymously published it as "A Methodist of the Church of England." See Lloyd, *Charles Wesley* for the history of Charles' more than thirty-year effort to keep the Methodists within the Church of England.

20. "On the Church," *AM* 9:50–51.

His magazine also carried two of his sermons, "Of the Church" and "On Schism," which further declared his opinion on the matter. In the sermons Wesley defined "the true members of the church of Christ" as those who do everything they can to promote unity and discourage strife within a church. To do otherwise—to stir up resentments between members—would inevitably lead to "the utter destruction, first of the power, and then of the very form of religion."[21]

Wesley closed the "Schism" sermon by giving thanks that he had no cause to withdraw from the national church. This church, he argued, neither required him to engage in practices that offended his religious sensibilities nor prevented him from carrying out his duties as an ordained priest. Therefore he declared, "I am now, and have been from my youth, a member and a minister of the Church of England. And I have no desire nor design to separate from it till my soul separates from my body."[22]

The December issue of the *Arminian Magazine* that year contains an article, "Of Separation from the Church," in which Wesley laid out the historical circumstances that had caused him to stray from Church of England polity (i.e., the practices of field preaching, society formation, conferencing, ordaining, and holding services during Church hours), and then argued that none of these actions violated church law. Furthermore, he stated, he had "no thought of [leaving the church]: I have many Objections against it."[23]

In addition to publicly broadcasting his commitment to remain a member of the Church of England, Wesley also addressed the issue in personal correspondence. In February 1786 he wrote to Thomas Taylor, a Methodist itinerant preacher, that he would not speculate on what the relations between the Methodists and the church would be after he died, for if he did, "I should probably shut myself up at Kingswood or Newcastle and leave you all to yourselves."[24]

21. Sermon 74, "On the Church," III.27, and Sermon 75, "On Schism," II.15, *Works* 3:55, 66.

22. Sermon 75, II.17, *Works* 3:67.

23. *AM* 9:675–78

24. *Letters*, 21 February 1786. A similar refusal to speculate on Methodist-Anglican relations after his death is found in "Of Separation from the Church": "'But for all this, is it not possible there may be such a Separation after you are dead?' Undoubtedly it is. But what I said at our first Conference above forty years ago, I say still, 'I dare not omit doing what good I can while I live, for fear of evils that may follow when I am dead.'" *AM* 9:678.

The following week he wrote to another Methodist preacher, Samuel Bardsley, "I believe I shall not separate from the Church of England til my soul separates from my body."[25] Similarly, a month later he wrote to his brother, "Indeed, I love the Church as sincerely as ever I did; and I tell our Societies everywhere, 'The Methodists will not leave the Church, at least while I live.'"[26]

In June, Wesley replied to concerned members of the Methodist Society in Dublin and assured their spokesman that his diversion from church polity would not lead to a schism: "We are members of the Church of England, we are no particular sect or party, we are friends to all, we quarrel with none for their opinions or mode of worship, we love those of the Church wherein we were brought up, but we impose them upon none; in some unessential circumstances we vary a little from the usual modes of worship, and we have several little prudential helps peculiar to ourselves; but still we do not, will not, dare not separate from the Church till we see other reasons than we have seen yet."[27]

Three months before the 1786 conference, Wesley wrote to his brother and informed him that in all probability eight or ten of the Methodist preachers would ask the conference to discuss a formal break with the church.[28] The Conference began on a Tuesday (July 25), and, as Wesley had anticipated, the question of separation was brought up during the Thursday session. After debate, the preachers unanimously voted that Methodism should stay where it was and remain what it was—a renewal movement associated with the form of the established church in England that promoted the power of religion among all Christians.

Judging by his correspondence, Charles thought the matter was finally settled. A few days after the vote was taken he wrote to his wife, "All agree to let my Brother and me remain in the Old Ship, till we get safe to land. He will (I am to think) be no more solicited to make a separation."[29] In the closing sermon for the conference, Charles predicted that a separation would happen but not until after he and his brother were dead.[30]

25. *Letters*, 4 March 1786. This repeats the assertion made in the "On Schism" sermon written 30 March 1786.

26. *Letters*, 6 April 1786.

27. *Letters*, 14 June 1786 to Henry Brooke and note 20.

28. *Letters*, 18 April 1786.

29. Tyson, *Assist Me to Proclaim*, 321.

30. The sermon speculates that two-thirds of the preachers and laity would break

John published a positive impression of the 1786 conference in his *Journal*: "Great had been the expectations of many that we should have warm debates. But by the mercy of God, we had none at all. Everything was transacted with great calmness, and we parted as we met, in peace and love."[31]

Doctrine, Spirit, Discipline

Maintaining this unity in love and confronting the tensions that continued to threaten Methodist harmony are the subjects of the article "Thoughts upon Methodism," which was written a few days after the close of the 1786 conference. The primary concern of the article is not the possibility that the Methodist movement would end, but that it would become "a dead sect, having the form of religion without the power." To prevent this from happening, Wesley advised his readers to hold fast to Methodist Doctrine, Spirit, and Discipline.

In order to better understand Wesley's advice, these components of Methodist Vitality are explained in the chapters that follow. Using "Thoughts upon Methodism" as a starting point, each chapter elaborates upon Wesley's definition of these terms. Chapter 2 recounts the developmental history of Methodist doctrine beginning with Wesley's early effort to become a faithful Christian and an effective priest. Chapter 3 focuses on Wesley's description of the changes that the power of religion produces within the soul. Chapter 4 discusses the disciplinary structure of Wesley's Methodism, and the methods and convictions that facilitated Methodist efforts to seek the power of religion. Taken together the chapters detail Wesley's opinions on who had the power of religion, what helped and hindered it, and how it should be pursued.

This book is written out of the conviction that as Wesley's heirs, Methodists should review his methods and compare them to their own attempts to effectively stir up within others a genuine desire for spiritual growth. For this reason, chapter 5 concludes with an evaluation of Wesley's advice for maintaining Methodist Vitality by adhering to Methodist Doctrine, Spirit, and Discipline, and discusses its potential viability as the foundation of an effective plan for ministry designed to meet the spiritual needs of today.

---

away and form an independent church. See Tyerman, *John Wesley* 3:478–79; and Jackson, *Charles Wesley*, 2:402–3.

31. Journal entries, 25–31 July 1786, *Works* 23:410–11.

Interest in revitalization programs is increasing as membership in American churches is decreasing. Too often these programs tend to be generically Protestant, meaning they can be implemented by churches of any denomination because the theology that informs the revitalization effort is limited to basic Christian tenets.

In contrast, Wesley's advice to his readers reflects a very specific theological viewpoint. He claimed God had entrusted the Methodists with a doctrinal teaching that would spread the form and power of religion wherever it was preached and taught. Methodists were distinctive, Wesley argued, and that distinctiveness kept them vital.

TWO

Ordering Methodist Doctrine

From the beginning the men and women sat apart, as they always did in the primitive church. And none were suffered to call any place their own, but the first-comers sat down first. They had no pews, and all the benches for rich and poor were of the same construction. Mr. Wesley began the service with a short prayer; then sung a hymn and preached (usually about half an hour), then sang a few verses of another hymn, and concluded with prayer. His constant doctrine was salvation by faith, preceded by repentance, and followed by holiness.

—*Thoughts upon Methodism*

Early Methodist worship services were both evocative and predictable. The Methodist preachers were trained to elicit an emotional response from their listeners by sticking to a preaching formula their leader had developed. In accordance with the Methodist preaching plan, upon first arriving at a society the preacher was to deliver a sermon that affirmed the love of God for sinful humanity. After relaying that message, the preacher was then to switch to sermons that convicted sinners and brought them to repentance. Once penitents began mourning their unrighteousness, they needed to hear sermons of assurance that told them their sins were forgiven by grace and through faith in Christ. Finally, the preacher's last sermons in the series were supposed to encourage the faithful to seek holiness of heart and life.[1]

By limiting his preaching to the doctrine of "salvation by faith, preceded by repentance, and followed by holiness," the typical Methodist

1. "To an Evangelical Layman," §§1–11, *Works* 26:482–84.

preacher could potentially run out of fresh sermon material in six to eight weeks. (Wesley himself once confided that if he stayed in one place for too long he feared he would preach himself and his congregation into a spiritual stupor.) This potential downside of the preaching plan was managed by rotating preachers among the Methodist Societies on a frequent basis.[2]

In spite of this drawback, the itinerant system of doctrinal preaching proved to be hugely effective. Early Methodist publications are full of testimonials from people who claimed to have had either no religion or only a lifeless, formal religion until they attended a Methodist preaching service and experienced the power of God's grace.

Wesley's claim that he constantly preached this doctrine is not entirely accurate, however. For while the religious advice he published for the members of the Methodist Societies reflects this doctrine, he did not consistently preach this order of the stages of salvation (repentance, then faith, then holiness) throughout his ministerial career. In fact, repentance and faith are rarely mentioned in his early sermons. It would be many years before his preaching method followed that order of salvation.

Wesley's conception of the means to salvation changed over his lifetime. As a child his definition of salvation amounted to little more than "keeping all the commandments of God," a standard that guided his outward behavior until he went to boarding school. While at Charterhouse his expectation for salvation was set at an even lower standard: "(1) not being so bad as other people; (2) having still a kindness for religion, and (3) reading the Bible, going to church, and saying my prayers."[3]

As a college student at Oxford University, Wesley continued to practice various forms of religion. He recited public and private prayers, read the Scriptures, and received communion three times a year. Despite these spiritual exercises, he characterized himself as a habitual sinner and infrequent repenter as an undergraduate. His occasional confessions of sin formed the foundation of his hope for salvation at this time.[4]

His understanding of salvation would undergo another change after he graduated from college, a shift in perspective that was greatly influenced by letters from home. While studying for a master's degree, Wesley deliberated on whether or not he should enter the ordained ministry. His parents,

2. Journal entry, 5 May 1784, *Works* 23:306; and Wesley to Samuel Walker, 3 September 1756, *Letters*.

3. Journal entry, 24 May 1738, §§1, 2, *Works* 18:242–43.

4. Journal entry, 24 May 1738, §3, *Works* 18:243.

Samuel and Susanna, wrote to him and offered him very different pieces of advice. His father thought that John should pray over the decision a while longer and in the meantime study ancient languages and read and reflect on Styan Thirlby's Latin and Greek edition of the fourth-century treatise *On the Priesthood* by St. Chrysostom.[5]

The letter from John's mother arrived a month later and, unlike her husband, she encouraged John to be ordained as soon as possible. Moreover, to prepare for ordination (and to improve his character) she suggested that John study books of practical divinity rather than the "trifling studies" she suspected her husband had recommended.[6] (A few weeks later his father wrote to say that he had changed his mind and decided that John could be ordained that summer.[7])

John followed both Samuel's and Susanna's advice as he prepared for the bishop's ordination examination. In his letters home he described the critical studies he was reading on the nature of faith and reason, on the doctrine of predestination, and on the heresy of skepticism. He also wrote to his parents and asked them for their opinions of two popular religious advice books.[8]

Motivated by the advice in these books, Wesley's letters demonstrate a new resolve to lead a more disciplined religious life. He began spending an hour or two in private devotions every day, he received communion every week, he tried to check his tendency towards any sinful behavior as soon as he became aware of it, and he prayed to be holy in his thoughts, words, and actions. These outward forms of godliness became the basis of his expectation of salvation during this period.[9]

Wesley was ordained as a deacon on September 19, 1725, and preached his first sermon on October 3rd. The sermons he wrote at this stage of his professional development do not include any reference to the religious advice books he was reading at this time. That advice would make its way into his preaching but not right away. Instead, the conception of salvation found in Wesley's early sermons exhibits evidence of an earlier influence.

5. Letter, 26 January 1725, *Works* 25:158.

6. Letter, 23 February 1725, *Works* 25:160.

7. Letter, 17 March 1725, *Works* 25:160.

8. Letters, 28 May; 18 June; 29 July; 18 August; 1 September; and 10 November 1725, *Works* 25:162–64, 167–70, 173–76, 178–81, 183.

9. Journal entry May 24, 1738, §4, *Works* 18:243–44.

From 1725 to 1729

Wesley preached in a variety of settings during this period, and he served in a range of capacities. As a new deacon of the Church of England he preached in a number of churches in and around Oxford. On March 17, 1726, he was elected a Fellow of Lincoln College, and even after assuming this academic role he continued to preach in Oxford churches and in country parishes. In 1727 he accepted his father's invitation to serve as curate in the Epworth parish, and the next year John was ordained priest on September 22, 1728. Wesley filled the curate position until November 1729, at which time he returned to Oxford after having been recalled to the University to fulfill the responsibilities of his fellowship.[10]

Throughout these changes in roles and locations, the themes of virtue and happiness are a constant in Wesley's sermons from 1725 to 1729. In these sermons Wesley preached the message that the cultivation of personal virtues is the only way to attain the thing that everyone wants (namely, happiness in this life) and the reward for becoming and remaining virtuous will be heaven or future happiness.[11] In Wesley's first sermons God is identified as the Infuser, Confirmer, and Perfecter of virtues while the Holy Spirit and the angels are portrayed as assistants that aid in the protection and retention of those virtues.[12]

The sermons' promise that salvation is given to those who "behave themselves on earth," as well as their emphasis on virtue as the means to happiness in this life and the next, is consistent with the educational philosophy Wesley encountered while at Oxford University.[13]

During the eighteenth century the curriculum at Christ Church exemplified the educational goal Aristotle advocated in his *Politics*—shaping the moral character of the young men who would become society's civic leaders. In 1720 when Wesley became a student at Christ Church, the legacy of Aristotle was still a principal influence on the college curriculum. Lectures and readings in logic, metaphysics, natural philosophy, and moral philosophy largely consisted of commentaries on the Aristotelian corpus.[14]

10. Outler, "An Introductory Comment" to Sermon 133, *Works* 4:204; Heitzenrater, "Oxford Methodists," 125, 431–36.

11. Sermons 133–138C, *Works* 4:211–13, 220, 222, 228, 234, 238, 250, 265.

12. Sermon 134, "Seek First the Kingdom," §6, and Sermon 135, "On Guardian Angels," II.8, *Works* 4:219, 231.

13. Sermon 134, §8, *Works* 4:220.

14. Sutherland and Mitchell, eds., *History of the University of Oxford*, 5:3, 472, 575.

Various features of the undergraduate program, Greek and Latin compositions, Aristotelian disputations, textbooks on logic, readings in classical literature, and lectures in mathematics, were supposed to develop the student's critical thinking skills and instill intellectual virtues (e.g., prudence, justice, fortitude, and temperance in reasoning).[15] Students were also assigned textbooks on moral philosophy and were required to read Greek and Latin classics that examined the causes and essential nature of morality from an Aristotelian perspective.[16]

The relationship between virtue and happiness is a recurring topic in Aristotelianism. For example, one commonly assigned undergraduate textbook on moral philosophy begins by defining happiness as the ultimate goal of human existence and then discusses how to cultivate the virtues that will cause one to be happy in this life and in the next. (The author of this text was Eustache de Saint-Paul [1573–1640], a seventeenth-century Aristotelian who left his professorship at the University of Paris to become a member of a Catholic reform movement within the Cistercian Order.)[17]

As an undergraduate Wesley was assigned an Eustache textbook that explains ethics in terms of the Aristotelian themes of virtue and happiness. Eustache began this treatment of moral philosophy with the declaration, "The end of all philosophy is human happiness, for in the eyes of the ancients nothing was a greater spur to philosophizing than the aim of becoming more blessed than other men. This happiness was taken to consist partly in the contemplation of the truth, and partly in action in accordance with virtue."[18] Eustache concluded the textbook with an examination of the virtues of prudence, justice, fortitude, and temperance.[19]

This Aristotelian teaching, not the religious advice books Wesley was reading, nor the order of repentance then faith then holiness, is reflected in the characterization of the way to salvation found in Wesley's first sermons. Apparently, some of his listeners found his preaching on virtue and

---

The attainment of virtues as the goal of an educated gentleman was a commonly held value by both British and American writers in the eighteenth century. Fiering, *Moral Philosophy*, 42.

15. Bill, *Christ Church*, 1–16, 245–97.

16. Ibid., 5, 275.

17. Fowler, *Descartes on the Human Soul*, 197 n. 23; Eustache de Saint-Paul, *Ethica*, 8; Marks, "General Introduction," xx, xxi; Fiering, *Moral Philosophy*, 89; and Bill, *Christ Church*, 298.

18. Eustache de Saint-Paul, "Compendium," 77, 78.

19. Ibid., *Ethica*, 1–27, 113–38. This reading assignment is mentioned in English, "John Wesley's Studies," 34.

happiness appealing. His diaries from 1725 to 1729 indicate that at least five churches invited him back as a preacher.[20] Yet despite these repeat invitations, Wesley expressed dissatisfaction with the response to his moral philosophy sermons:

> From the year 1725 to 1729 I preached much, but saw no fruit of my labour. Indeed it could not be that I should; for I neither laid the foundation of repentance, nor of believing the gospel; taking it for granted, that all to whom I preached were believers, and that many of them "needed no repentance."[21]

In retrospect, Wesley concluded that preaching about virtues had not led to the moral reform of his listeners. This insight occurred to him many years later, however, for the sermons from the next period of his ministry show that he continued to preach on virtue and happiness, though evidence of his reading of religious advice books does begin to show up in his preaching.

From 1729 to 1734

When Wesley returned to Oxford in 1729 to fulfill his duties as a Fellow of Lincoln College, his brother Charles was a student at Christ Church, and John became the leader of a small group that Charles had started. Together the members followed the forms of religion that were typical of the religious society movement within the Church of England, though Wesley's group added a few practices that were unique to their circumstances. The friends attended communion services at the University, conducted their own worship services at the Oxford prisons, organized primary education classes for poor children, studied classical literature, Scripture, and religious tracts, and offered mutual encouragement to one another as they attempted to make the love of God and Neighbor the orienting virtue of their lives.

In addition to these extracurricular activities, Wesley also gave a weekly theological lecture (in Greek and based on the Greek Testament) to all the undergraduates of Lincoln College, moderated their Latin disputations, and met with the pupils he tutored at least six days a week to evaluate their intellectual and moral development.[22] He also delivered nine

20. Outler, "Introduction," *Works* 1:29.

21. "The Principles of a Methodist Farther Explained," VI.1, *Works* 9:222.

22. Overton, *John Wesley*, 23; and Heitzenrater, "Oxford Methodists," 98, 109.

university sermons while in residence at Oxford, a number that is higher than average, and which has been interpreted as an indication of Wesley's popularity as a preacher.[23]

He still preached about virtue and happiness during this period, although a new theme does appear—the image of God. The 1729–1734 sermons detail the pre-Fall characteristics of the *imago Dei*, the effect of Adam's disobedience on these characteristics, and the steps necessary to renew the image God.

The characteristics of the *imago Dei* mentioned in Wesley's sermons (i.e., understanding, will, affections, and liberty) are the same as the faculties of the soul identified in Eustache's moral philosophy.[24] As originally created, these faculties worked with Adam's body in a harmonious and error-free way. His thinking was clear and accurate. His desires and emotions were inspired by love. His choices were free and indifferent.[25]

The liberty of free choice, however, was the cause of Adam's downfall. By defying God's command and eating the forbidden fruit, Adam ingested a poison that disrupted his bodily functions, altered the soul's faculties, and defaced the *imago Dei*. The juice from the fruit caused blockages to form throughout Adam's body, which eventually lead to his death.

These obstructions affected every aspect of the soul's functions. They interfered with the brain's inner workings, which in turn affected the soul's capacity for reasoning. Without the ability to form accurate judgments, the understanding was unable to guide the will. Consequently, the will was overwhelmed by sinful feelings, which caused Adam to choose vice over virtue. This chain of cause and effect ultimately led to the loss of happiness for both Adam and his posterity.[26]

Wesley reassured his listeners that the solution for this human condition has been provided by God, who sent Christ to teach humanity the steps they had to follow in order to recover what has been lost. These steps involve renewing the *imago Dei* by correcting the faculties of the soul. First, the virtue of humility was to be cultivated. This virtue could reform the faculty of the understanding and aid the progression towards salvation

23. Outler, "Introduction," *Works* 1:2, 109–10.

24. Eustache de Saint-Paul, "Compendium," 78–80.

25. Sermon 141, "The Image of God," I.1–4, *Works* 4:293–95. These faculties of the soul can also be found in the Christ Church textbook *An Exposition of the Creed*, by John Pearson. For example see the 1701 edition, 395–96.

26. Sermon 141, II.1–5, and Sermon 146, "The One Thing Needful," I.2, I.4, *Works* 4:297–99, 354.

because humility imparted an accurate sense of one's fallen condition and need for religion.[27]

The second step to renewing the *imago Dei* involved reforming the will and affections by means of the virtue of charity. Wesley used the verbs "root out," "put away," "resolve," "stifle," and "lay aside" to describe this step. An act of the will is required, an intentional choice to seek happiness in the things that are eternal rather than in the things of this world, and to fix the affections on imitating Christ by practicing love of God and neighbor.[28]

Once the faculties of understanding, will, and affections are corrected and regulated, the liberty of the soul will no longer be influenced by vice but will be free to follow the will of God. This newfound freedom produces a feeling of present happiness and an anticipation of future happiness. To recover a sense of liberty, "to throw off every chain, every passion and desire that does not suit an angelical nature," is to be born again.[29]

Even though occasional reference is made to the need for God's grace to assist the soul in its effort to be virtuous and happy, the overwhelming focus of Wesley's argument is on the need to imitate Christ through an exertion of willpower. The role of grace in the order of salvation is left a divine mystery.[30]

Wesley attributed his new focus on the imitation of Christ to the study of Scripture he engaged in during this period. For several hours every day, Wesley read the Bible in the original languages and consulted commentaries. (A commentary published around this time, written by the Puritan minister Matthew Henry—one referenced by both John and his brother Charles later in their careers—also contains the same connection between imitating Christ and renewing the image of God found in Wesley's sermons.[31])

27. Sermon 141, III.1, and Sermon 142, "The Wisdom of Winning Souls," II.1, *Works* 4:299–300, 311–12.

28. Sermon 141, III.2, Sermon 142, II, and Sermon 146, I.1–III.3, *Works* 4:300, 312–14, 352–59. A specific example of charity to the neighbor is given in Sermon 143, "Public Diversions Denounced," 328. Renewal of the *imago Dei* through love of God is explained in Sermon 144, "The Love of God."

29. Sermon 141, III.3, Sermon 145, "In Earth as in Heaven," and Sermon 146, I.3, II.2, *Works* 4:300–301, 349–50, 354–55.

30. Sermon 139, "On the Sabbath," I.3, II.2, III.1, Sermon 140, "The Promise of Understanding," I.3, and Sermon 146, II.3, II.5, *Works* 4:270, 274–75, 284, 356–57.

31. "The Principles of a Methodist," §16, *Works* 9:57; Henry, *Old and New Testament*, 6:192; Wesley, *Plain Account of Christian Perfection*, §5, *Works* (Jackson) 11:367; and Routley, "Charles Wesley and Matthew Henry," 345–51.

The argument that by virtuously following Christ the *imago Dei* will be recovered can also be found in the religious advice books that Wesley was reading. The 1677 English edition of the Thomas à Kempis classic *The Imitation of Christ* and works by William Law and Henry Scougal argue that humanity must pattern themselves after the example of Christ in order to renew the fallen image.[32]

Additionally, many Anglican theologians from the Carolinian Age used the recovery of the *imago Dei* as a metaphor for salvation.[33] Wesley's undergraduate textbook on Anglican theology contains the teaching that humanity was created in the image of God and must imitate God by being holy.[34] Also, he would have come across this message in the sermons of Bishop William Beveridge, which he read in 1726.[35]

Wesley's new emphasis on the image of God can be seen in the conception of religion that he defended at this time. As a young man he may have conceived of Christianity as "outward decency" and "the bare saying over so many prayers morning and evening, in public or in private," but that was in the past. Now he described religion as "a constant ruling habit of soul; a renewal of our minds in the image of God; a recovery of the divine likeness; a still-increasing conformity of heart and life to the pattern of our most holy Redeemer."[36]

The relationship between the renewed *imago Dei* and holiness of heart and life becomes more prominent in Wesley's sermons during this period; however, preaching on the human predicament and the need for renewal did not seem to produce much of a change in the lives of his listeners:

> From the year 1729 to 1734, laying a deeper foundation of repentance, I saw a little fruit. But it was only a little; and no wonder: For I did not preach faith in the blood of the covenant.[37]

The need for repentance is never mentioned in these sermons on the Fall and the renewal of the *imago Dei*, and faith is only referred to twice.[38]

32. Law, *Practical Treatise*, 461; Scougal, *Life of God in the Soul of Man*, 5, 12; and à Kempis, *Christian's Pattern*, iii.

33. McIntosh, "Nature and Design of Christianity in John Wesley's Early Theology," 55.

34. Pearson, *Exposition of the Creed*, 30.

35. Heitzenrater, "Oxford Methodists," 497.

36. Wesley to Richard Morgan, Sen., 15 January 1734, *Works* 25:368–69.

37. "Principles," VI.1(2), *Works* 9:222–23.

38. Sermon 140, III.2, and Sermon 146, III.3, *Works* 4:288, 359.

Instead, the path to salvation laid out in the 1729–1734 sermons is still focused on the cultivation of virtues, though the theme of holiness does become more prominent during this period, a trend that continues into the next phase of Wesley's development as a preacher.

From 1734 to 1738

Wesley's circumstances underwent a major alteration during this period. In 1734 he was a fellow of Lincoln College and leader of a small religious society made up of university students. Four years later he was in London explaining to the trustees of the Georgia colony the reasons why he had abandoned his post as priest of the Savannah parish. Every transition, from academic grove to colonial wilderness to metropolitan commons, was highly contentious.

The first person to suggest to John that it was time for him to leave Oxford was his father. In October 1734 Samuel shared with John his wish to resign the Epworth parish and have John succeed him. Samuel was dying, and even though such an arrangement would ensure that Susanna could continue to reside in the rectory after the death of her husband, John's first impulse was to reject the offer. He contended that he needed the support of his circle of friends at Oxford (known by outsiders by a variety of names, including "The Methodists") in order to live a Christ-like life.[39]

A tense correspondence ensued between Samuel, his eldest son Samuel Jr., and John. The nature of John's duty was debated by the three Wesleys. The Samuels stressed the duty of a son and of a priest. John emphasized the duty of all Christians to imitate Christ, and contended that in his case the responsibilities of the parish would detract from that higher calling. The monastic-like atmosphere of the University supported his efforts to become holy, whereas the daily demands of parishioners would undermine that goal, he argued.[40]

John's resolve wavered only when Samuel was on his deathbed. Upon returning home and seeing his dying father, John attempted to secure the Epworth living but was unsuccessful. Another priest moved into the rectory after Samuel died, and Susanna went to live with one of her daughters.[41]

39. Heitzenrater, "Oxford Methodists," 29, 30, 283–89.

40. Ibid., 303–6.

41. Ibid., 308–11.

Not long after this familial disagreement, John was invited to become a missionary in the American colonies. Trustees of the Georgia colony enticed Wesley with visions of converting the indigenous peoples who lived near the Savannah settlement. Intrigued by the idea of establishing a church in a primitive environment, Wesley accepted the offer with his mother's blessing. He was accompanied on this adventure by his brother Charles, Benjamin Ingham (another Oxford Methodist), and Ingham's friend Charles Delamotte.[42]

Books on primitive Christianity had been on the Oxford Methodist reading list for years prior to this mission. One of his correspondents even used the term as a nickname for Wesley. His interest in the first centuries of the church was influenced by his association with a subgroup of Anglicans called the Nonjurors, who advocated for the incorporation of ancient Christian practices into the worship services of the established church.[43] The opportunity to go to America was a chance to turn theory into reality.

Unfortunately for Wesley, his ministry in Georgia did not go as planned. Upon arrival he discovered that the trustees of the colony needed him to become the priest of the Savannah parish. His conversion of the American tribes delayed, Wesley tried to establish primitive Christianity among the colonists by strictly adhering to the sacramental rubrics of the Church of England and by teaching his parishioners the forms of religion practiced by the Oxford Methodists.

Wesley's sermons from the Georgia mission reflect his high aspirations for the religious lives of the colonists. Unlike the previous sermons these do not place an equal emphasis on all of the faculties of the soul. The need to reform the will by making the glory of God the single intention of every activity is the main subject of the 1736 and 1737 sermons. This emphasis reflects the influence that religious advice books written by Jeremy Taylor, Thomas à Kempis, and William Law were having on Wesley's conception of salvation.

Taylor's advice in the book *The Rule and Exercises of Holy Living* convinced him that he should dedicate every thought, word, and action to God. After reading *The Imitation of Christ*, he was persuaded that he also needed to offer his will to God and make glorifying God his main purpose in life.[44]

42. Ibid., 317–31.

43. Campbell, *John Wesley and Christian Antiquity*, 28–33.

44. *Plain Account of Christian Perfection*, §§2, 3, *Works* (Jackson) 11:366–67.

In William Law, a popular Nonjuror author, Wesley encountered a merging of his aim to be single-minded with his interest in primitive Christianity. The Christians of his day were not as pious as early Christians, Law suggested in his religious advice books, because they lacked the single intention to glorify God in every activity. Law admonished his readers to "have this intention to please God in all your actions as the happiest and best thing in the world," not just while attending Sunday worship, but in the daily affairs of life, as well.[45]

"To improve in holiness, in the love of God and thy neighbor" was Wesley's definition of the Single Intention. Such an aim pleases God and should be the Christian's motive for every thought, word, action, design, and resolution, Wesley told his new flock. This was to be the primary goal of the colonists in every part of their lives, from religious activities to their business, refreshments, diversions, and conversations.[46]

Wesley promised his listeners that if they followed these instructions and focused their outward activities on this single intention, then they would find favor with God, and the Holy Spirit would so purify their understanding and affections that they would be filled with hope, peace, joy, and love. Through this divine assistance they would be transformed "till what was but now a weak, foolish, wavering, sinful creature, be filled with all the fullness of God!"[47] All it took to get this transformation process started was willpower.

In another sermon from this period, Wesley reminded the congregation of the duties they had to perform in order to receive eternal life: obey the commandments, attend public worship, pray, study Scripture, fast, receive the Eucharist, do good, practice self-denial, and love God and neighbor.[48] This list of duties is almost identical to the advice given by Jeremy Taylor, except that the instructions in *Holy Living* include repentance and faith among the forms of religion that should be done to the glory of God in this life in order to partake of future glory in the next.[49]

When looking back on this period of his ministry, Wesley sounds uncertain of the extent to which his sermons inspired his American parishioners to single-mindedly exert their willpower to the glory of God:

45. Law, *Serious Call*, 13–14.

46. Sermon 148, "A Single Intention," II.2–6, *Works* 4:374–76.

47. Sermon 148, II.9, *Works* 4:376–77.

48. Sermon 149, "On Love," §4, II.2, 3, *Works* 4:381, 383.

49. Taylor, *Holy Living*, 2–3, 60, 228–360. The internal duty of Hope and external duty of Festival observation are also mentioned by Taylor.

> From 1734 to 1738, speaking more of faith in Christ, I saw more fruit of my preaching, and visiting from house to house, than ever I had done before; though I know not if any of those who were outwardly reformed were inwardly and thoroughly converted to God.[50]

Wesley's doubts about the depth of reform in his converts reflect how his ministry in Georgia ended. The experiment in primitive Christianity fell apart when Wesley was accused of disrespecting the head bailiff of Savannah. Wesley had had amorous inclinations towards the magistrate's niece, Sophia Hopkey, and he was shocked when she became engaged to a man in whom she had previously denied having any romantic interest.

Sophia's attendance at public prayers and communion became less regular after she married, and she discontinued her habit of fasting. Subsequently, Wesley wrote to Sophia and informed her that this lack of religious discipline, along with the fact that she had lied to him about her true marital aspirations, were grounds for barring her from communion. Following the rubrics of the church, when Sophia came to the altar, Wesley explained to her in a hushed tone that she was required to notify him beforehand of her intention to commune. Moreover, he explained that in order to receive the communion elements, she first had to confess her transgressions and repent.[51]

Warrants were issued for Wesley's arrest after this sacramental rebuff. Sophia and her husband filed suit against Wesley for defamation of character and sued for one thousand pounds sterling in damages. Sophia's uncle accused Wesley of multiple acts of ecclesiastical irregularity.[52] The complaints were reviewed by a grand jury, and a majority found sufficient evidence to indict Wesley on ten counts of misconduct. Concurrently, a minority report was submitted by twelve members of the grand jury, who concluded that the charges against Wesley were groundless and were merely an act of revenge instigated by the vindictive head bailiff.[53]

Wesley had criticized the colonial magistrates' handling of two previous cases, and when his repeated requests for a court date were denied, he questioned whether or not he would receive a fair hearing from the

50. "Principles," VI.1(3), *Works* 9:223.

51. 5 July 1737, letter to Sophia Williamson; Journal entry 7 August 1737; and "Affidavit of Margaret Burnside," *Works* 18:524, 534–35, 549.

52. Journal entry 9 August 1737; and "List of Grievances," *Works* 18:537, 555–56.

53. Journal entries 22 August–7 October 1737, *Works* 18:190–93.

Savannah justice system.[54] Since the indictment against him had been referred to the Trustees of Georgia, Wesley decided to return to England and offer the Board a defense of his ministry and a report on the condition of the colony. On December 2, 1737, after evening prayers and in violation of a travel ban, Wesley jumped bail, boarded a ship in Charleston, and arrived in England two months later.

He had been forced to end his primitive Christianity experiment in America; however, his effort to revive the church was about to assume a new form.

From 1738 to 1746

Wesley had multiple meetings with the trustees of Georgia, recounted his version of the events that led to his departure, and told them his impression of the state of the colony. Finding evidence of fault on both sides, the board accepted Wesley's resignation, and resolved to investigate the conduct of the head bailiff.[55]

While he was in London for these meetings, Wesley became acquainted with a group of Moravian missionaries. He had sailed to America with members of this German church, had lived with them until the Savannah rectory was available, and had held numerous religious conversations with them about their beliefs.

Peter Böhler became Wesley's Moravian conversation partner in England. At first Wesley did not understand Böhler's theology, or what he meant when he said Wesley's philosophy must be *excoquenda* (to be purged away or tempered by heat). Eventually, Böhler convinced him that salvation was achieved by grace through faith in Christ and not by the virtuous intentions Wesley had been trying to cultivate for the last thirteen years. Wesley's subsequent study of Scripture confirmed Böhler's Moravian interpretation of happiness as an instantaneous sense of assurance that past sins were forgiven, as well as the Moravian version of holiness as freedom from sin.[56]

After a month of conversations with Böhler and other Moravians, Wesley stopped preaching the virtues of a Single Intention attained through

54. Hammond, "Restoring Primitive Christianity," 251–59.

55. Journal entries 15–22 February 1738, *Works* 18:224–26.

56. Journal entries 18 February; 4, 6, 23 March; 22, 23 April; and 24 May 1738, §12, *Works* 18:226, 228, 232–34, 248.

the exertion of willpower and instead began to preach salvation by grace through faith, even though he had not had the type of religious experience that Böhler described. Wesley's *Journal* from this period recounts the feelings of heaviness and disappointment he endured as church after church rejected his new definition of salvation and barred him from their pulpits.

For two and a half months, Wesley practiced his usual forms of religion, wrestled with temptations, and prayed for faith in Christ until, finally, at a religious society meeting on Aldersgate street, Wesley instantaneously experienced happiness and holiness as defined by Böhler. What has come to be known as Wesley's Aldersgate experience occurred while he was listening to a reading of *A Methodical Preface to Romans*, a book that contained Martin Luther's argument that through faith in Christ the heart is renewed by the work of the Holy Spirit and only then can the heart love and willingly obey the moral law. In describing that moment, Wesley wrote:

> I felt my heart strangely warmed. I felt I did trust in Christ, Christ alone for salvation, and an assurance was given me that he had taken away my sins, even mine, and saved me from the law of sin and death.
>
> I began to pray with all my might for those who had in a more especial manner despitefully used me and persecuted me. I then testified openly to all there what I now first felt in my heart.[57]

His ability to pray for his enemies in the face of the rejection of his ministry by the American colonists and by the London churches is a poignant testimony to the immediate impact that his encounter with the power of religion had on him.

He still preached on primitive Christianity, virtue, holiness, the renewal of the *imago Dei*, and happiness. After his Aldersgate experience, however, Wesley is critical of his earlier characterizations of the Christian life. Moral philosophy is considered a lower degree of faith in his subsequent sermons. The person who relies on willpower to help him or her please God in all areas of life is labeled an "almost Christian," not a real Christian.[58]

In the 1738–1746 sermons his description of holy living sets up his call to repentance. For example, in his 1744 University sermon, Wesley began by describing the virtues of the early Christians, and then asked the congregation of Oxford men to compare themselves to the first members

57. Journal entry 24 May §§14, 15, *Works* 18:250.

58. Sermon 2, I.1–13, II.8, *Works* 1:131–36, 140.

of the church. Are the fruits of the Spirit evident in their lives? Do the university officials reflect the image of God? Does the faculty promote love of God and neighbor? Are the students and tutors virtuous and holy? If not, then they must pray to God and request the gift of faith.[59]

Faith is defined in the sermons from this period as a conviction that God graciously offers forgiveness of sins to everyone who repents and trusts in Christ for atonement.[60] Assurance immediately follows faith and is attributed to the Holy Spirit, who bears witness that the penitent has been reconciled to God.[61]

After repentance and faith, believers progress to holiness. Wesley used metaphors of growth and maturation to illustrate the nature of Christian holiness. From a newborn babe nursing on the milk of the gospel, the Christian will eventually grow into "the stature of the fullness of Christ" (Eph 4:13).[62] The babe in Christ is graciously enabled to resist temptations and does not commit sinful acts. With growth in grace, the compulsion of sinful thoughts and emotions lessens until finally they cease to determine the behavior of the adult Christian.[63]

Extrapolating from his vision of holy individuals, Wesley imagined what societies would be like when holiness encompassed the earth. Brutality will end then; hostilities between nations, cities, neighbors, and family members will cease. Everyone will have the necessities of life, thus negating motivations to extort, rob, plunder, or swindle. The golden rule will guide all interactions. Kindness and truthfulness will characterize all conversations.[64]

This new emphasis upon holiness as freedom from sin (reflecting the Moravian perspective on holiness as dominion over sin) is a notable difference between these sermons and the ones Wesley wrote before 1738. His earlier sermons merely state that the faculty of liberty is renewed following the restoration of the *imago Dei* without any further explanation. In contrast, the post-Aldersgate sermons teach that by faith Christians are set

59. Sermon 4, "Scriptural Christianity," *Works* 1:161–80.

60. Sermon 1, "Salvation by Faith," §3, I.3, I.5, Sermon 2, II.9, and Sermon 4, I.1, *Works* 1:118, 120–21, 141, 161.

61. Sermon 1, Sermon 2, Sermon 4, and Sermon 110, "Free Grace," §14, *Works* 1:122–23, 128, 141, 161–63, and 3:549.

62. Sermon 1, II.7, Sermon 40, "Christian Perfection," II.1, *Works* 1:124–25; 2:105.

63. Sermon 40, II.21, *Works* 2:117.

64. Sermon 4, III, *Works* 1:169–72.

free from the power of sin. They are so transformed by the power of grace that as a result they no longer succumb to sinful desires, habits, emotions, or intentions.[65]

Once Wesley started preaching salvation by grace through faith evidenced in assurance and freedom, the response was dramatic:

> From 1738 to this time, speaking continually of Jesus Christ, laying Him only for the foundation of the whole building, making him all in all, the first and the last; preaching only on this plan, "The kingdom of God is at hand; repent ye, and believe the gospel"; the "word of God ran" as fire among the stubble; it was "glorified" more and more; multitudes crying out, "What must we do to be saved?" and afterwards witnessing, "By grace we are saved through faith."[66]

The claim that "multitudes" were following Wesley's post-Aldersgate order of salvation (repentance then faith then holiness) is no exaggeration. During this period, Wesley imitated the example of his Oxford Methodist colleague George Whitefield and preached not only in churches and to religious societies, but also at outdoor venues that accommodated thousands of listeners.

Wesley and his brother Charles joined the ranks of eighteenth-century itinerants who traveled throughout England, Ireland, Scotland, and Wales organizing Evangelical revivals. John tried to form an association of priests sympathetic to the movement, but theological differences caused the Wesleys to part ways with the Moravians and also with the Calvinists, who were led instead by Whitefield.

Despite these breakups, more and more people joined the religious societies affiliated with the Wesleys. To accommodate the larger gatherings, the Methodists began to build preaching houses, first in Bristol and London and later throughout the British Isles. The increase in the number of and distance between preaching engagements necessitated that the brothers accept the help of lay preachers to meet the growing demand. By 1744 a conference of preachers, ordained and lay, working in connection with the Wesleys, had been established. Two years later that connection would be organized into seven preaching circuits.

65. Sermon 1, II.5, II.6, Sermon 2, II.6, and Sermon 4, I.6, I.7, *Works* 1:123–24, 139, 163–64.

66. Principles," VI.1(4), *Works* 9:223.

From 1746 to 1763

During this period the doctrinal standard for Methodist preaching was officially established. Between 1746 and 1763 Wesley published four volumes of sermons and three volumes of New Testament commentary in an attempt to provide theological guidance to his untrained lay preachers. In 1763 the Methodist Conference required that all sermons delivered in Methodist preaching houses adhere to the doctrinal teachings found in these sermons and commentaries. The order of salvation is the primary focus of these institutionally endorsed statements of Methodist Doctrine, and this order can be divided into five stages: Asleep, Almost, Awake, Abiding, and Altogether.

Preventing the Asleep

Wesley used the story of Eutychus, the young man who sat on a window ledge listening to Paul preach only to doze off and fall out the window (Acts 20:7–13), to illustrate the predicament of the spiritually Asleep. Those in this state are unaware that they are at spiritual risk. Ignorantly joyful, confident, and self-satisfied, the Asleep think they have no reason to fear God's judgment. Some are atheists, while others believe in God, but make no effort to live holy lives because they trust God to be merciful to them in spite of their sinfulness.[67]

Although they do not have faith in God or Christ, the grace of God still has influences them. Wesley used the term "preventing" to describe the activity of grace in those who are Asleep. Preventing grace affects them in two ways. First, it is the voice of conscience that sways the Asleep towards moral behavior and away from vice. Second, preventing grace makes it possible for the Asleep to respond to the gospel. Sometimes they react with joy and sometimes with fear, and usually the emotion is short-lived.[68] However, if that feeling of awe and fear should persist, then grace has begun to exert a different influence on them, one which Wesley termed "convincing grace."

67. Sermon 9, "Spirit of Bondage and of Adoption," §§5–8, Sermon 19, "The Great Privilege of those that are born of God," I.6–I.8, and Sermon 45, "The New Birth," II.4, *Works* 1:250–55, 434; 2:192; *Notes* Acts 20:12; Eph 5:14; 2 Tim 3:26.

68. Sermon 9, IV.2, and Sermon 12, "The Witness of Our Own Spirit," §5, *Works* 1:265, 302; *Notes* Matt 13:20; Rom 2:14.

Convincing the Almost

The Almost are snapped out of their false sense of confidence, recognize that their thoughts, words, and actions do not conform to God's moral law, feel shame, repent of their rebellion, and desire to be obedient. Their inability to change their ways and consistently follow God's commandments increases their feelings of helplessness, guilt, and fear.[69]

Cornelius is the biblical equivalent of someone who is Almost a Christian. Cornelius feared God, offered prayers, and gave alms to the poor before he had faith in Christ (Acts 10:1–48). Based on this example, Wesley concluded that even a heathen "that first reverences God, as great, wise, good, the cause, end, and governor of all things; and secondly, from this awful regard to him, not only avoids all known evil, but endeavours, according to the best light he has, to do all things well; *is accepted of him*—Through Christ, though he knows him not."[70]

Justifying the Awake

When Cornelius heard Peter's testimony he believed the gospel, had faith in Christ, and entered the Awake stage of salvation. The Methodists taught that this saving faith was the gift of God. By grace through faith, the Awake realize that their justification is accomplished for them through Christ and not on account of anything that they have done. By grace through faith, they are assured that Christ died for them, their sins are forgiven, and they are reconciled to God. The Awake still feel inward sinful impulses, but by God's grace these inclinations do not lead to deliberate sinful actions, and they have faith that one day they will be liberated from the power of sin.[71]

Wesley taught that at the same moment sinners are justified, they also experience the power of religion and are born again. The process of sanctification begins at that point and continues in the next stage of salvation.[72]

69. Sermon 7, "The Way to the Kingdom," II.1, II.7, Sermon 9, II.7–II.10, and Sermon 21, I.4–I.9, *Works* 1:225, 229, 258–60, 278, 477–80.

70. *Notes* Acts 10:4, 35.

71. Sermon 3, "Awake, Thou that Sleepest," II.2, Sermon 5, II.1, Sermon 7, II.9, Sermon 8, "The First-fruits of the Spirit," II.5, Sermon 9, III.4–III.7, Sermon 12, §15, Sermon 17, "The Circumcision of the Heart," I.7, and Sermon 18, "The Marks of the New Birth," I.3, *Works* 1:147, 187, 230, 239, 262, 309, 405, 418–19; *Notes* John 1:12–13; 10:17; Acts 26:29; Rom 5:1; 6:1–23; 13:11; 1 Cor 15:34; Titus 3:5.

72. Sermon 45, IV.3, *Works* 2:198.

Sanctifying the Abiding

Wesley defined sanctification as "being made actually just and righteous." As with justification, this stage of salvation is a work of grace and is not accomplished through human effort. Through grace as the power of the Holy Spirit, the faculties of the soul are transformed, the *imago Dei* restored, and the Abiding are enabled to understand, love, and obey God. The fruits of the Spirit are outwardly evident in their conduct and attitudes, especially in the love they show their neighbors. Because they are aware of the sinful impulses that remain within them, the Abiding know they cannot reform their character on their own, but need God's help if they are to perfectly love God and their neighbor.[73] Through the means of grace (such as prayer and the reading of Scripture), those in this stage abide in Christ and await full deliverance from the power of sin.[74]

The Philippians are the biblical example of the Abiding (Phil 1:6). Paul knew the members of the church in Philippi had been justified, and he was certain that the work of sanctification continued in them and would be perfected by grace.[75]

Perfecting the Altogether

John the beloved disciple is the biblical example of the Altogether.[76] Those in the Altogether stage are thoroughly free from the power of sin and no longer have sin-filled habits. God's perfecting grace enables them to obey all the commandments and, in effect, turns commands into promises. Whatever God requires of Christians, God promises to accomplish for Christians at this stage of salvation. This includes the command to love God with all the heart, soul, and mind (Matt 22:37), to love the neighbor (Matt 19:19), to pray without ceasing (1 Thess 5:17), and to be holy in all conversations (1 Pet 1:15–16).[77]

73. Sermon 8, I.3–I.6, III.5, Sermon 9, III.6, Sermon 21, I.13, *Works* 1:187, 236–37, 247, 262, 482.

74. *Notes* John 15:6–10; 1 John 1:13–14.

75. *Notes* Phil 1:6.

76. "Thoughts [on Christian Perfection]," *SOSO* 4:253.

77. Sermon 25, "Sermon on the Mount, V," II.2, 3; Sermon 40, "Christian Perfection," *Works* 1:554–55; 2:99–121; *SOSO* 4:252; and *Notes* Matt 5:48. Non-doctrinal writings that support this teaching can be found in Sermon 76, "On Perfection," II.1, 5, 11, *Works* 3:76–77, 80; and Letter, 20 December 1751, §§13–17, 26:484–85.

The expectation that grace could work so powerfully and transformationally that it could entirely fill the soul and crowd out impulses to sin was a doctrine that had been uniquely entrusted to the Methodists, Wesley claimed. He even went so far as to assert that the reason God had raised up the Methodist movement was so that they could teach others the doctrine of entire sanctification. No sermon series was complete until the preacher encouraged the congregation to press on to experience the full power of religion, which would give them total dominion over sin and make them perfect observers of God's commandments.[78]

Repentance–Faith–Holiness

The order of salvation taught in Wesley's doctrinal writings can be diagramed thus:

God:	Preventing Grace	Convincing Grace	Justifying Grace	Sanctifying Grace	Perfecting Grace
Human:	Asleep	Almost	Awake	Abiding	Altogether
Religion:	Form of Religion		Form of Religion Power of Religion		

God's grace initiates and sustains the salvation process. The Asleep and Almost experience this grace, typically as conveyed through various forms of religion. Grace prevents the Asleep from remaining ignorant of their sin and convinces the Almost to repent. The Awake receive the power of religion when they are given the gift of faith in Christ; they grow in this grace by continuing to use the forms of religion while in the Abiding stage, and they await a further experience of the power of religion that allows them to reach the goal of the Christian life and become Altogether Christians.

Wesley contrasted the Methodist order of salvation with another that appeared in religious advice books written for members of the Church of England beginning in 1645. In *A Practical Catechism*, the Anglican priest Henry Hammond argued that Christians had a duty to lead holy lives and

78. Wesley to Robert Carr Brackenbury, 15 September 1790, *Letters*.

that this dutiful obedience to God qualified them for pardon.[79] Therefore, sanctification must occur first, according to Hammond, and only then is justification warranted.

Hammond linked this order of salvation to the Adamic Covenant.[80] Every Christian was baptized into this covenant, he contended, and if its conditions were met (i.e., "*faith, hope, charity, self-denial, repentance,* and the rest"), then God would grant salvation to the holy.[81]

Fulfilling the terms of the covenant is possible because Christ's precepts for Christian living are reasonable. The new life in Christ described in the New Testament is "agreeable to the rational soul." Everyone, from the least educated to the most, recognizes that the morality required by God is a sensible and good way to live.[82] (In other words, common sense should persuade everyone to behave in a manner consistent with the moral law.)

If common sense fails, there is no reason for fear or despair to weaken one's resolve. Grace is also promised in the Adamic covenant, a gracious power that enables an individual to lead, if not a sin-free life, then at least one that meets the covenant's moral expectations. Besides, the promise of mercy is offered to those who, in spite of their sincere efforts to perform their Christian duties and lead a righteous life, still occasionally slip back into sinful habits. This offer of mercy is solely contingent upon the repentance of the lapsed sinner.[83]

The religious advice book *Holy Living* by Jeremy Taylor was influenced by Hammond's catechism and follows the same order of salvation. Taylor taught that as holy duties are performed and sinful habits rooted out, the probability of pardon increases. Pardon can never be taken for granted, however. Degeneration is expected and is a cause for concern "because every new sin and every great declining from the ways of God is still a degree of new danger, and hath increased God's anger, and hath made him more uneasy to grant pardon."[84]

79. Hammond, *Practicall Catechisme* (1645), 285.

80. Hammond's Covenant Theology was a reaction to Puritan Covenant Theology. For this historical context see Lettinga, "Covenant Theology Turned Upside Down"; McGiffert, "Henry Hammond and Covenant Theology"; and Packer, *Transformation of Anglicanism.*

81. Hammond, *Practicall Catechisme* (1645), 13, 48–112.

82. Ibid., 5.

83. Ibid., 6, 7.

84. Taylor, *Holy Living*, 340–42.

The last half of the seventeenth century saw the release of more publications (most notably the seemingly ubiquitous *The Whole Duty of Man* by Richard Allestree) that stressed the Adamic covenant's order of salvation, the difficulty of amending one's life, and the uncertainty of retaining one's pardon.[85]

Wesley challenged this widely held conception of salvation on three fronts. First, God's covenant with Adam had been made before the Fall, in a state of innocence that has been lost, thus making it impossible for anyone to enter into the terms of that original agreement. Second, unlike Hammond, who assumed God would accept sincere if imperfect efforts to become holy, Wesley argued that fulfilling Adam's covenantal obligation required unerring obedience to God's moral law. Therefore, moral perfection, not moral sincerity, was necessary to be saved under the terms of the original covenant.[86] Third, Wesley labeled Hammond's position a covenant of works and contrasted it with the covenant of grace, which is made with sinners, not the already dutiful. Meeting the conditions of the grace covenant requires repentance from sin and faith in Christ, not sinless obedience. When these conditions are met, God pardons the unrighteous.[87]

Wesley and the Oxford Methodists had studied and tried to pattern their spiritual practices after the instructions given by Hammond, Taylor, Allestree, and other authors of religious advice books. These efforts had given Wesley a form of godliness, but not the renewal of the *imago Dei* that his readings had taught him to expect. In frustration he wondered why his sincere desire to be outwardly holy did not move God to make him inwardly holy.[88]

Only after he started preaching "salvation by faith preceded by repentance and followed by holiness" did he experience the power of religion, and it was then that his ministry became effective. From that point on he advised others how they could experience the power that could renew the *imago Dei*. His advice included a challenge to press on towards the goal of the Christian life, and he equated that goal with the Spirit of his movement. For the movement to remain vital, his assistants would have to preach the

85. Purcell, "Useful Weapons," 124–47; Tennant, "Christopher Smart and *The Whole Duty of Man*," 63–78; Elmen, "Richard Allestree," 19–27; and Sharpe, "Social Control in Early Modern England," 1:37–54.

86. Sermon 6, "The Righteousness of Faith," II.2–II.4, *Works* 1:210–11.

87. Sermon 5, III.1–III.7, and Sermon 6, I.8–I.11, *Works* 1:190–97, 207–8.

88. Martha Wesley to John Wesley, 10 January 1730, *Works* 25:242.

doctrine of entire sanctification and encourage the Methodists to use the form of religion until they grew in faith and reflected the characteristics of an Altogether Christian.

THREE

Experiencing the Methodist Spirit

What was their fundamental doctrine? That the Bible is the whole and sole rule both of Christian faith and practice. Hence they learned: (1) That religion is an inward principle; that it is no other than the mind that was in Christ; or in other words, the renewal of the soul after the image of God, in righteousness and true holiness. (2) That this can never be wrought in us but by the power of the Holy Ghost. (3) That we receive this and every other blessing merely for the sake of Christ; and, (4) that whosoever hath the mind that was in Christ, the same is our brother, and sister, and mother.

—*Thoughts upon Methodism*

METHODIST DOCTRINE FOLLOWED A predictable path to a preferred end—salvation by faith preceded by repentance and succeeded by an inward experience of the power of religion that renewed the *imago Dei* and patterned it after the example set by Christ. This was the goal of the Christian life according to Wesley, to be born again as a new creation by grace through faith, and this goal represented the spirit of Methodism for him. Hitting that target required an encounter with the power of God's grace that turned one into a new creature inwardly (characterized by "new life, new senses, new faculties, new affections, new appetites, new ideas and conceptions") as well as outwardly (represented by new actions and new conversations).[1]

Neither a religion of opinions, nor a religion of outward worship, nor a religion of good works could satisfy the aspirations of the Methodists because the religion of the new creature was a religion of the heart. For

1. *Notes* 2 Cor 5:17.

Wesley, heart religion was synonymous with the Altogether stage of salvation, and its chief characteristics were holiness, happiness, and certainty.[2]

The Methodists looked for evidence of these characteristics in themselves and in others in order to determine who was a new creature and who had yet to be born anew. To help his followers make this determination, Wesley printed a range of publications that described the traits of an Altogether Christian, and that explained the emotions and experiences that people typically underwent as the power of religion moved them through the various stages of salvation on their way to becoming inwardly and outwardly Christ-like.

The New Soul

Wesley taught that the new creature has a different perception of reality than do those with little or no faith. The new creature "lives, as it were, in a new world. God, men, the whole creation, heaven, earth, and all therein, appear in a new light, and stand related to him in a new manner, since he was created anew in Christ Jesus."[3] This faith perspective is radically unlike the viewpoint of the spiritually asleep.

In his sermons Wesley argued that the Asleep are in a spiritual situation comparable to that of an unborn child. The baby *in utero* has eyes, ears, and a nose, however none of the sense organs allows the little one to perceive the reality that exists outside the womb. Analogously, the Asleep are surrounded by a divine reality that they cannot perceive because they do not have faith.[4]

Wesley based his definition of faith on Hebrews 11:1, "Faith is the assurance of things hoped for, the evidence of things not seen." Faith, Wesley argued, provided the soul with evidence of the supernatural by means of spiritual senses, which he compared to the physical senses that provided evidence of the natural world to the soul.[5]

2. Preface to Sermons, §6; Sermon 7, I.6, Sermon 18, "The Marks of the New Birth," I.2, 3, Sermon 36, "The Law Established through Faith, II," I.5, Sermon 120, "The Unity of the Divine Being," §15, *Works* 1:106, 220–21, 418; 2:36; 4:66; "An Earnest Appeal to Men of Reason and Religion," §4 *Works* 11:46; Journal entry 17 July 1755, *Works* 21:20; Wesley to John Erskine, 24 April 1765; and Wesley to James Knox, 30 May 1765, *Letters*.

3. *Notes* 2 Cor 5:17.

4. Sermon 19, "The Great Privilege of Those Born of God," I.3–I.10, Sermon 45, II.4–II.5, and Sermon 130, "On Living without God," §16, *Works* 1:433–35; 2:192–94; 4:176.

5. Sermon 12, §8 and Sermon 106, I.10, 12, *Works* 1: 251, 255, 260, 304; 3:497–98.

The spiritual senses are dormant in the Asleep; at the Almost stage they are stimulated just enough to cause a feeling of conviction; and they are fully opened when faith is given to the Awake through the operation of the Holy Spirit. Like a newborn baby sensing the world for the first time, the Awake are born again by the Spirit, and their newly regenerated and functional spiritual senses take in impressions of the divine realm, which is now directly experienced by the new creatures. The regeneration of the spiritual senses transforms the understanding, will, affections, and liberty of the Awake, although Wesley did not claim to know in what manner or precisely how the Spirit worked upon the soul.[6]

The New Understanding

Wesley drew upon his Aristotelian education to describe the effect that the spiritual senses have upon the soul's faculty for understanding. In his undergraduate textbook on logic, reasoning is described as a thinking process that is dependent on input from the physical senses. The soul apprehends the physical world through the body's sensory organs, ideas about what the senses perceive are then formed, and the soul arrives at judgments about the nature of reality based upon these ideas. Lastly, the soul compares judgments and deliberates in order to determine which ones accurately reflect reality and which are in error.[7]

Because the physical senses cannot pick up on immaterial realities, the soul cannot rely upon them to help it gain an accurate understanding of God and the things of God. Only the regeneration of the spiritual senses can provide the soul with impressions of the divine realm. Once sensory impulses of a spiritual nature are available, the invisible, spiritual, and eternal worlds become as knowable to the soul as the physical world.

Such things as the human soul, angels, and demons are examples of the unseen things that Wesley associated with the invisible world understood by faith. Because of the spiritual senses, the soul also perceives that there is a God and understands that God is the Creator, Sustainer, and Governor, who is omnipresent, omnipotent, loving, wise, just, merciful, and

6. Sermon 10, I.12, Sermon 43, II.1, Sermon 117, §13 "Farther Appeal, Part I," I.6, and "A Letter to the Bishop of Gloucester," III.(II).11, *Works* 1:276; 2:161; 4:35; 11:108, 534; *Letters* 17 November 1760.

7. Matthews, "Study in the Theology of John Wesley," 136–52, 157.

holy. Likewise, belief in the Trinity and the incarnation is possible because the soul apprehends these truths by faith.[8]

Wesley equated the spiritual world discerned by faith with "the kingdom of God within." The conviction of the Awake that Christ loves them and redeems them is based on their new capacity to grasp this truth by faith. Through the spiritual senses the assurance of the Spirit testifying that one has been adopted as a child of God can also be detected by the soul. The Abiding's discernment that maintaining a state of spiritual health depends upon the sustained working of the Holy Spirit, and the trust of the Altogether that Christ has cleansed them from all unrighteousness is also made possible by the spiritual senses.[9]

"A view of things to come" in the eternal world is given by faith, as well. The soul knows that the righteous dead will be received into paradise by the angels, and once there will join the saints and see Christ face to face. Faith also provides evidence of the truth that upon death the unrighteous will be seized by the demons and will suffer unending torment. In addition, the soul has a clear idea of the Last Judgment and grasps the everlasting consequence of preferring good and shunning evil.[10]

New Affections, Will, and Liberty

The experience of faith has an impact on the other faculties of the soul, too. The new creature's understanding impacts the affections, will, and liberty, a transformation of the soul that makes it possible for the justified to mature in faith and reach the Altogether stage of holiness, happiness, and certainty.[11]

The knowledge of God's pardoning love causes the new creature to love God in response (1 John 4:19). This emotional reaction to grace transforms the affections, which in the Almost state had been dominated by a fear of God as judge and punisher of sin. After the spiritual senses are opened, the feelings of love, peace, and joy eventually become the primary emotional characteristics of the Altogether (Rom 14:17).[12] Faith saves them

8. Sermon 39, I.13, and Sermon 117, §§3–7, *Works* 2:87; 4:30–32.

9. Sermon 117, §§12, 13, and "Earnest Appeal," §§6–8, *Works* 4:34, 35; 11:46, 47; and *Notes* 1 Thess 5:6.

10. Sermon 117, §§8–11, *Works* 4:32–34.

11. Sermon 10, I.8, 9, II.11, Sermon 62, "The End of Christ's Coming," III.1, "Farther Appeal, I" IV.1, *Works* 1:274–75, 282–83; 2:481; 11:132–33.

12. Sermon 130, "On Living without God," §11, "Earnest Appeal," §57, *Works* 4:173; 11:67.

from disquietude, and they become content and at peace with their life situations. Their sense of the eternal world makes them feel joyful and hopeful that they will reach that desired end (Phil 3:14).[13]

Knowledge of the eternal world has an effect on the faculty of the will, too. When the new creature understands there is more to life than what may be perceived by the physical senses it begins to desire things of eternal significance rather than the transitory things of the material world, and it bases its choices in this life on whether or not a word or action will prepare the soul for heaven.[14]

The more the new creature exercises its spiritual senses by using them to discern what is spiritually good and what is spiritually evil, and then acts on that discernment by choosing what is good and resisting what is evil, the more it prefers the good, until eventually this preference becomes an ingrained habit of the will.[15]

The spiritual senses also help the will make choices that are in conformity with God's will. For Wesley discerning God's will was a straightforward task: "The will of God is our sanctification," which meant that as long as a decision contributed to human betterment it was consistent with God's will. Because of its capacity for reasoning, humanity is capable of judging which choices conformed to this divine intention, Wesley argued, particularly when it is aided by grace. The spiritual senses provide even more assurance that the will is following a course of action in keeping with God's will by giving the will a sense of the Holy Spirit's promptings and by causing the new creature to feel peace of mind when it makes a faithful choice.[16]

The good intentions of the will can now be actualized because the regeneration of the spiritual senses also restores the faculty of liberty. Unlike some of his contemporaries, who argued that the soul did not have freedom of action (either because it was dependant upon the body or because its actions were predestined by God), Wesley contended that those who can perceive God do have a measure of liberty restored to them because their actions are no longer slavish reactions to sinful impulses. Their sense of the invisible world makes it possible for them to know and obey God's commands. Furthermore, their increasing sense of God's love can have such a

13. Sermon 7, II.11, "Earnest Appeal," §8, *Works* 1:230–31; 11:47.

14. Sermon 62, III.2, Sermon 119, §14, *Works* 2:481; 4:55.

15. "The Character of a Methodist," §11, *Works* 9:38; and *Notes* Heb 5:14.

16. Sermon 37, "The Nature of Enthusiasm," §§21–25, *Works* 2:54, 55.

profound influence on new creatures that divine love is able to govern and regulate all their inward and outward behaviors.[17]

Wesley's publications include descriptions of the soul changes that he associated with the opening of the spiritual senses. In *Hymns and Sacred Poems*, for instance, the characteristic emotions of new creatures, who have an inward experience of grace and faith that transforms the functions of their souls, are detailed in a Charles Wesley hymn "Describing Formal Religion," which John first published in 1742:

My sin and nakedness
I studied to disguise;
Spoke to my soul a flattering peace,
And put out mine own eyes;
In fig-leaves I appeared,
Nor with my form would part;
But still retained a conscience seared,
A hard, deceitful heart.

. . . .

But Oh! The jealous God
In my behalf came down;
Jesus himself the stronger showed,
And claimed me for his own.
My spirit he alarmed
And brought into distress;
He shook, and bound the strong-man, armed
In his self-righteousness.
Faded my virtuous show,
My form without the power;
The sin-convincing Spirit blew,
And blasted every flower.
My mouth was stopped, and shame
Covered my guilty face;
I fell on the atoning Lamb,
And I was saved by grace.[18]

17. Sermon 19, par. 10, "Character," §12, and "The Principles of a Methodist," §9, *Works* 9:39, 53; "Thoughts [on Christian Perfection]," *SOSO* 4:241; "Thoughts Upon Necessity," §IV.4, 5, and "A Thought on Necessity," §VI, *Works* (Jackson) 10:473–74, 478–79.

18. Hymn 90, vv. 5, 7, and 8, *Works* 7:192–93.

The hymn explains that the Asleep could maintain a false sense of security as long as the spiritual senses were closed. This state of spiritual blindness comes to an end when divine power begins to work within the soul and confronts it with its sins. From feelings of alarm, shame, and guilt, the Almost moves on to a sense of salvation only when trust is placed in Christ rather than in the form of religion.

The faith experience of someone progressing through the Awake to the Altogether stages is illustrated in two Charles Wesley hymns "Describing Inward Religion," the first of which John published in 1749:

We who in Christ believe
That he for us hath died,
We all his unknown peace receive,
And feel his blood applied:
Exults our rising soul,
Disburdened of her load,
And swells, unutterably full
Of glory, and of God.
. . . .
The meek and lowly heart,
Which in our Saviour was,
He doth to us impart,
And signs us with his cross:
Our nature's turned, our mind
Transformed in all its powers,
And both the witnesses are joined,
The Spirit of God with ours.
Whate'er our pardoning Lord
Commands, we gladly do,
And guided by his sacred Word,
We all his steps pursue:
His glory is our design,
We live our God to please,
And rise, with filial fear divine,
To perfect holiness.[19]

When the powers of the mind are transformed through the opening of the spiritual senses, the Awake can detect the invisible things of God (in

19. Hymn 93, vv. 2, 5, and 6, *Works* 7:196–98.

this hymn the unseen atoning blood of Christ) and discern the spiritual world within as the Spirit witnesses to the new creature assurance of its salvation. The Abiding's sense of the divine fills them with peace and holy awe. They are enabled to follow God's moral law and glorify God in every thought, word, and action as they pursue the Altogether stage.

The sense of the eternal world is described in a second inward religion hymn written by Charles Wesley, which John published in July 1740:

> To him that in thy name believes
> Eternal life with thee is given;
> Into himself he all receives—
> Pardon, and happiness, and heaven.
> The things unknown to feeble sense,
> Unseen by reason's glimmering ray,
> With strong, commanding evidence
> Their heavenly origin display.
> Faith lends its realizing light,
> The clouds disperse, the shadows fly;
> Th' Invisible appears in sight,
> And God is seen by mortal eye.[20]

This hymn is an edited version of an eighty-five-stanza poem on the eleventh chapter of the book of Hebrews published by Charles two months before John came out with his redaction. In the hymn the definitive evidence of God and the things of God provided by faith is contrasted with the feeble religious insights gained through the exercise of reason.

This insight into the supernatural causes the new creature to develop new character traits. The hymn mentions happiness as one such trait; John's publications also frequently describe holiness and certainty as characteristic of the Altogether Christian.

New Traits

Wesley advised the Methodists that they could expect to feel the lure of sinful impulses decrease and a spiritual appetite to imitate Christ increase as they progressed towards the Altogether stage and their sense of the invisible, spiritual, and eternal worlds intensified. When this occurred, nothing

20. Hymn 92, vv.4–6, *Works* 7:194–95.

worldly would satisfy their craving to be made Christ-like, nor could outward forms of religion quench their longing to be renewed in the image of God. Only the holiness imparted by the power of religion would make them happy and confident.

Holiness of Heart and Life

For Wesley, Christian holiness consisted of two components—"having the mind that was in Christ" (1 Cor 2:16), or holiness of heart, and "walking as Christ walked" (1 John 2:6), or holiness of life.[21]

Wesley conceived of holiness of heart as an internal disposition of the soul, especially the faculty of the affections. He taught that unholy affections, such as anger and pride, would be expelled when the spiritual senses were opened and the power of God's love filled the soul. This sense of God's love would then inspire all the other holy affections of the new creature: "joy, peace, long-suffering, gentleness, goodness, fidelity, meekness, temperance, and whatsoever else is lovely or praiseworthy."[22]

Love of God is inseparably linked to love for one's neighbor in the Methodist spirit. Wesley described this regard for others as "the most tender goodwill, the most earnest and cordial affection, the most inflamed desires of preventing or removing all evil and of procuring for him every possible good . . . Him thou shalt 'love as thyself'; with the same invariable thirst after his happiness in every kind, the same unwearied care to screen him from whatever might grieve or hurt either his soul or body."[23]

By grace through faith, the new creature is enabled to feel mercy for others, to love the neighbor to the same degree that it loves itself. This love kindly reassures those who suffer, is patient in the face of shortcomings, provocations, and cruelties, rejoices at the happiness of others, is circumspect, humble, courteous and unsuspicious, grieves over iniquity but

21. Sermon 22, II.1–6, and Sermon 33, III.9, *Works* 1: 495–98, 697.

22. Sermon 2, II.1, Sermon 8, "The First-fruits of the Spirit," I.6, Sermon 22, II.1, Sermon 26, "Sermon on the Mount, VI," §1, Sermon 127, "On the Wedding Garment," §17, "Earnest Appeal," §98, and "A Farther Appeal to Men of Reason and Religion, Part III," I.5, *Works* 1:137, 237, 495, 573; 4:147; 11:89, 275. The *Appeals* list other examples of holy affections based on Matt 5:12; 1 Cor 13:7; Phil 4:8, 11; Col 3:12; 1 Thess 5:16, 18; and 1 Pet 1:8, 5:7 (88, 269, 275 notes).

23. Sermon 7, I.8, I.9, *Works* 1: 221–22.

remains hopeful, seeks the salvation of every soul, and delights to discover holiness in members of another religious party.[24]

When every unholy affection is displaced from the soul, and God is loved with all the heart, soul, mind, and strength, and the neighbor is loved as the self, then the Altogether stage has been reached and the believer is "pure in heart" (Matt 5:8). For Wesley this love for God and others is more than a private emotion; it also inspires personal action. Holiness of life is possible when (by grace through faith) the will is transformed, becomes singular and reflects a pure intention to glorify God in every thought, word, and deed.[25]

The notion that holiness of life is a natural extension of holiness of heart is consistent with the doctrinal homilies of the Church of England, which state that "a loving heart to obey [God's] commandments" is one of the first fruits of justifying faith. For Wesley this teaching implied that the capacity to love grows and increases whenever the will exerts itself by abstaining from activities contrary to God's moral law and by following the golden rule.[26]

Wesley frequently repeated his expectation that their experience of the power of religion would inspire the Methodists to use every talent they possessed (whether physical, spiritual, mental, financial, or social) to help others. He gave examples of the types of good works he expected his followers to perform, which included providing for the physical needs of even the enemy, visiting the sick and the prisoner, lovingly admonishing sinful behavior, and carrying on other edifying conversations. These good deeds were manifestations of the holy affections that fill the soul after it has been renewed by grace, he explained. Such works do not merit salvation; they are observable indicators that salvation has occurred and that God is at work in the soul.[27]

24. Sermon 22, III.3–III.18, and Sermon 23, III.2–III.13, *Works* 1: 499–509, 520–30.

25. Sermon 23, I.2, "Earnest Appeal," §57, and Journal entry 18 April 1760, *Works* 1:510–11; 11:68; 21:250; and *Notes* Gal 5:6.

26. Sermon 2, II.6, Sermon 30, "Sermon on the Mount, X," §27, and Sermon 127, §17, *Works* 1:139, 663; 4:147; and *Notes* 1 Cor 7:19.

27. Sermon 1, III.2, Sermon 22, III.1, Sermon 23, II.4–II.7, Sermon 85, "On Working Out Our Own Salvation," I.2, and Sermon 114, "On the Death of John Fletcher," I.3, *Works* 1:125, 499, 518–20; 3:202–3, 612–13.

Present and Future Happiness

Only when the new creature receives the gift of inward and outward holiness by grace through faith will it know true happiness. Faith in Christ, not the cultivation of virtues, is the path to happiness to which Wesley pointed his readers after his Aldersgate experience. As the affections are reformed after the mind of Christ and the will is conformed to the example of Christ's life, feelings of contentment increase until ultimately faith becomes sight and present happiness yields to eternal happiness.[28]

Christian happiness, as defined by Wesley, did not exclude sorrow. The love the Altogether feel for the neighbor may cause them to experience compassion or a sense of shared suffering with those under affliction. The love the Altogether feel for God may lead to persecution, given that the unrighteous hate the holy, Wesley warned, just as they hated Christ. This hatred can take the form of character assassination; it can cause strains in relationships with friends and family members, as well as economic deprivation, and perhaps even the loss of "health, liberty, and life."[29]

Mistreatment, affronts, and malicious gossip can be borne with grace, Wesley advised, when the power of God's love fills the soul. Love is patient, or long-suffering—one interpretation of *makrothumos* (1 Cor 13:4) that Wesley used in his sermons. To be long-suffering means that, by God's grace, the Altogether can tolerate being ill-treated by others, are mild when speaking to them, kind when interacting with them, and are able to pray for them (Matt 5:44).[30]

Another reason the Altogether can retain their sense of happiness while enduring trials is because they sense that God is providently directing their persecutor's animosity and channeling it into actions that will best promote God's glory and their own growth in grace.[31]

28. Sermon 7, I.9, 10, Sermon 28, §5, Sermon 59, "God's Love to Fallen Man," I.10, Sermon 77, "Spiritual Worship," II.5, 6, Sermon 84, "The Important Question," III.3, Sermon 90, "An Israelite Indeed," I.2, Sermon 120, §§11, 17, and Sermon 127, §19, *Works* 1:222–23, 615; 2:431; 3:96, 97, 189, 283; 4:64, 67, 148.

29. Sermon 23, III.1–11, Sermon 84, III.6, Sermon 59, I.6–10 and "Advice to the People called Methodists," 19, *Works* 1:520–27; 2:428–31; 3:191–92; 9:129; and *Notes* Matt 6;10, 11; John 15:19–21; Gal 4:29; 2 Tim 3:12; and 1 John 3:14.

30. Sermon 22, III.3, Sermon 23, III.13, Sermon 149, II.4, "Character," §9, and "Advice," §26, *Works* 1:499, 529; 4:383; 9:38, 131.

31. Sermon 23, III.5, *Works* 1:523.

The connection between holiness, happiness, and suffering is explored in many of Wesley's publications, especially when he wrote about the relationship between the Altogether stage and future salvation. Wesley predicted that there would be two categories of Christians in heaven. One group would be made up of Altogether Christians while the other consisted of those who were content with the form and did not pursue the power of religion. The latter group was justified by faith, lived blamelessly, did good works, and practiced the form of religion; nevertheless these people constituted a "lower order of Christians," in Wesley's opinion, who wrote that "they will not have so high a place in heaven as they would have had if they had chosen the better part."[32] Only those with holy affections, and pure intentions, and no appetite for worldly things will relish and enjoy the employments of heaven.[33]

The afflictions, persecutions, and temptations that the Altogether suffer in this life are not indications that they are in the lower order of Christians. On the contrary, because the reward they will receive in heaven is in proportion to the stage of salvation they reach in this life, those who retain their trust in God in spite of hardships will gain a greater heavenly reward than those who never strengthened their faith by exercising it in the midst of struggles.[34]

What is more, the endurance of trials increases feelings of happiness. Wesley reassured his friend Hannah Ball, "Do you not remember that fine remark in the *Christian Instructions*, 'Nothing is more profitable to the soul than to be censured for a good action which we have done with a single eye.'" Suffering that causes bodily harm or renders the Altogether incapable of performing their duty is the exception to this rule. Excluding these extreme forms of persecution, Wesley taught that godly sorrow could be a blessing if the consolation and assistance of divine grace is perceived in the midst of the trial.[35]

32. Sermon 89, "The More Excellent Way," §5, *Works* 3:265–66. Comparable sentiments expressed in Sermon 22, *Works* 1:494 and Journal entry 25 January 1739, *Works* 19:32.

33. Sermon 94, "On Family Religion," II.2, Sermon 124, "Human Life a Dream," §§8, 11, and Sermon 127, §10, *Works* 3:337; 4:113, 115, 144; *Notes* Col 1:12; and *Letters* to Elizabeth Hardy, 5 April 1758.

34. Sermon 23, III.11, Sermon 47, V.2, Sermon 56, II.3, Sermon 59, I.6–8, II.11, and Sermon 129, II.6, *Works* 1:527; 2:234, 399, 428–32; 4:167, and *Notes*, Rom 8:31–39. Sermon 58, §5, §§7–10 *Works* 2:417–19; and *Notes* Rom 8:29–30; 1 Pet 1:2; 4:13.

35. 30 May 1772, *Letters*. The positive effect of suffering is also mentioned in Sermon

The religious advice book Wesley quoted in his letter to Hannah Ball, *Christian Instructions*, contains other maxims on the spiritual benefits of long-suffering; edited by Wesley, the book is an extract of an extract. The original work was a two-volume collection of letters written by Jean du Vergier de Hauranne, a Catholic priest and the leader of the Jansenist movement in France. Robert Arnauld d'Andilly—a French nobleman and Jansenist who lived in a monastic-like community with other laity at the monastery of Port-Royal-des-Champ, where Hauranne was the spiritual director—redacted the letters down to a single volume and numbered each paragraph in his edition. Even after all his paraphrasing, d'Andilly's 374-page volume still contained 1063 paragraphs of religious advice.

According to Wesley's book ledger, he had acquired a copy of d'Andilly's extract by 1733. In 1760, Wesley published an extract of d'Andilly, which reduced the paragraphs by more than a third, to 336 numbered sentences. This fifty-four page work, titled *Christian Instructions, extracted from a late French Author* was published in volume four of Wesley's collection of doctrinal sermons after his tract, "Thoughts on Christian Perfection."[36]

Wesley further reduced the length of his Hauranne extract on two more occasions. In 1763 Wesley published *Farther Thoughts upon Christian Perfection*, and at the end of this pamphlet he included a nine-page, nine-section synthesis of "Christian Instructions." The synthesis has no title and is set off from the *Farther Thoughts* by an introduction: "Most of the preceding Advices are strongly enforced in the following Reflections: Which I recommend to your deep and frequent Consideration, next to Holy Scriptures."

Wesley's synthesis of the Hauranne letters next appeared in *A Plain Account of Christian Perfection*, though once again slightly edited until at this point it contained only eight sections. The sentiments expressed in section two of the *Plain Account* version draw from five different Hauranne-inspired letters, which Wesley merged together into a succinct statement on the spiritual benefit of persecution.

Insults and losses are to be accepted with thankfulness, Wesley stated, using a close English translation of d'Andilly's French. Experiencing and

18, "The Marks of the New Birth," II.5, Sermon 57, "On the Fall of Man," II.8, Sermon 59, "God's Love to Fallen Man," I.7, and Sermon 84, III.6 *Works* 1:424–25; 2:411, 428–29; 3:191–92.

36. Heitzenrater, "Oxford Methodists," 495.

then bearing affliction is a sign that God's grace is at work in one's life. Most important of all, enduring persecution promotes Christ-likeness.[37]

Sections three and four of Wesley's extract recommend suffering quietly, without "a sharp or peevish word," even for undeserved attacks, because suffering only becomes profitable when faced with humility, patience, and love.[38]

Though technically not an original writing, given the level of translating, editing, and synthesizing evident in the work, it is fair to claim that this advice reflects Wesley's perspective, especially since Wesley's extract is consistent with statements in his sermons about the contribution that long-suffering can make to the pursuit of holiness and happiness.

For example, in Sermon 47 he wrote that even though distressing circumstances might bring about a temptation to doubt the goodness of God, trials can also be a time of testing that strengthens faith (1 Pet 1:7). As Wesley put it, "sanctified afflictions have (through the grace of God) an immediate and direct tendency to holiness. Through the operation of his Spirit they humble more and more, and abase the soul before God. They calm and meeken our turbulent spirit, tame the fierceness of our nature, soften our obstinacy and self-will, crucify us to the world, and bring us to expect all our strength from, and to seek all our happiness in, God."[39]

Wesley did not downplay the grievous extent to which people can suffer from a prolonged illness or because of impoverishment or in response to the death of a loved one. What he denied was that physical pain or emotional sorrow would inevitably cause a loss of faith. On the contrary, he went so far as to claim that suffering may be necessary for a time in order to increase faith, produce holiness and happiness, and to "brighten our crown" in glory.[40] The Methodist spirit is reflected in the new creature who aspires for heaven and seeks it by grace through faith no matter what persecutions arise in the course of that pursuit.

Given the emphasis Wesley placed on the relationship between the Altogether stage and future salvation, an additional stage must be added to those already comprised in the doctrinal Order of Salvation:

37. *Plain Account of Christian Perfection*, (§1.), *Works* (Jackson) 11:436.

38. Ibid., (§3., §4.), *Works* (Jackson) 11:437.

39. Sermon 47, "Heaviness through Manifold Temptations," III.1–III.3, IV.1–IV.5, and Sermon 48, "Self-denial," I.12 *Works* 2:226–28, 231–33, 245.

40. Sermon 47, V.2, *Works* 2:234.

God:	Preventing Grace	Convincing Grace	Justifying Grace	Sanctifying Grace	Perfecting Grace	Glorifying Grace
Human:	Asleep	Almost	Awake	Abiding	Altogether	Angelic

Such a diagram fits with Wesley's occasional reference to the order of salvation as "Pardon, Holiness, Glory."[41]

By trusting God in the midst of trials, Wesley reasoned, the Altogether grow in grace in this life and prepare for their future life in glory. He viewed both the Altogether and Angelic stages as dynamic rather than static, finished states. Increasing in knowledge and love while on earth readies the Altogether for eternal increases in holiness and happiness in the Angelic stage.[42]

A Certain Faith

The new creature's sense of the invisible, spiritual, and eternal worlds also increases its feelings of certainty in religious matters. The perception of the divine realm communicated by the spiritual senses convinces the new creature of the truth of religious teachings, and this certitude causes them to progressively feel more confident—confident they have been pardoned, sure they have been sanctified, and finally certain they will be received into heaven.

Wesley printed the testimonials of preachers and laity that recounted the religious experiences of individual Methodists as they passed through the various stages of salvation on their way to the Angelic stage. These publications provided examples for others to emulate and from which they could take comfort. The narratives described what the justification and sanctification processes felt like, how family and friends typically reacted to Methodist conversions, and how various trials and temptations were

41. "The Early Conferences," (1746), [§35], *Works* 10:175.

42. Sermon 5, II.5, Sermon 6, I.5, Sermon 30, §27, Sermon 42, "Satan's Devices," II.4, Sermon 58, "On Predestination," §§11, 16, Sermon 59, "God's Love to Fallen Man," II.16, Sermon 116, "What is Man?" §13, Sermon 119, "Walking by Sight and Walking by Faith," §18, and Sermon 132, "On Faith," §6, *Works* 1:190, 206, 663; 2:149–50, 419, 421, 435; 4:25, 57, 58, 192; and *Notes* Rom 8:30; 10:10; 13:11; 1 Cor 15:44; 2 Thess 2:13, 14; and 2 Pet 3:18.

endured as Methodists sought to be made holy, happy, and confident by the power of religion through faith in Christ.

Grace Prevents William Ferguson

William Ferguson attended the Presbyterian Church in Scotland as a child, but his involvement with organized religion ended when he became a teenager. About that time his family moved to a town where most of their neighbors were engaged in the illegal trafficking of smuggled goods. Rather than imitating the example of Christ, young William adopted the habits of those around him. Cursing, swearing, lying, drinking, dancing, playing cards, and mocking the pious were his preferred diversions during the years leading up to his twentieth birthday.

Any delusion of indestructibility he might have harbored as a teenager was challenged on three separate occasions—twice when he came close to drowning and once when a soldier pressed the barrel of a gun into William's chest and threatened to shoot him in the heart. Each of these brushes with death had a sobering effect on him at first; however, none of them led to a lasting change. He wrote, "I was serious for a while after [nearly drowning]. But I then got into laughing, trifling company; and my seriousness soon wore off . . . The thought of instant death [by gunshot] shocked me much. But this too I stifled by drinking and dancing . . . So I continued fast asleep in the devil's arms."

An imaginary, sudden-death scenario shook him awake in a way that these actual brushes with death had not. One day while at work and daydreaming about that evening's plans to drink, dance, and play the fiddle, he heard a voice ask him, "What if thou shouldest drop down dead in the midst of the dance! Wouldest thou go to heaven?" He admitted to himself that he was "not fit for heaven," and would most likely be sent to hell. In that moment, "light broke in: I was filled with horror: I saw myself hanging over the mouth of hell, by the brittle thread of life!" On this occasion the shock was not suppressed, and not long after his religious awakening he chose to move away from his parents and friends and seek out a community where his new faith would be nourished. His search ended when he met John Wesley and joined the Methodists.[43]

43. "William Ferguson," *AM* 5:292–97, 346–51.

Grace Convinces John Pawson

Unlike William Ferguson, John Pawson did not go through a rebellious phase. Pawson was raised in the Church of England, and as a teenager he attended a religious society affiliated with the church. Unsurprisingly, given his long-standing ties to the established church, he was at first suspicious of Methodism. Later, after he became acquainted with several Methodists and began reading evangelical sermons, his opinion of them improved and he started attending Methodist preaching services.

His parents objected to his involvement with the Methodists, issued warnings that his reputation would be harmed and that his construction business would suffer if he became a Methodist, and threatened to disinherit him. Pawson endured almost two years of arguments, tears, and accusations before he eventually pacified his parents' misgivings. (After this reconciliation, his parents plus five other members of the family joined a Methodist society.)

Even with the support of his family, Pawson still described his faith as "dull and unaffected" at this time, and he prayed for a sense of contrition. A Methodist service in a neighboring village was the setting for his experience of convincing grace: "in the beginning of the service, the power of God came mightily upon me and many others. All of a sudden my heart was like melting wax, my soul was distressed above measure. I cried aloud with an exceeding bitter cry; the trouble and anguish of spirit that I laboured under far exceeding all description." Pawson remained in this state of conviction for several months before finally experiencing assurance of forgiveness.[44]

Grace Justifies Sarah Clay

Sarah Clay also spent a considerable amount of time at the Almost stage before she experienced forgiveness of sins. She first heard Wesley preach in 1739 at her parish church, St. Mary Islington in London. (In June 1738, Charles Wesley had been invited to become the curate of this parish, and John preached there several times over the course of the next ten months.) Sarah enjoyed the sermon so much that she went again the next Sunday, and even though she started to feel convicted by Wesley's messages, the feeling did not put her off church. On the contrary, she became a regular churchgoer.

44. Pawson, *Short Account*, 31–34.

Not everyone in the Islington church appreciated Methodist doctrine, however. In April 1739 Charles was banned from the pulpit, as was George Whitefield, and later John was also barred from preaching there. After that, Sarah's church attendance became less regular and her sense of conviction diminished.

Soon after the Islington ban, Sarah heard that Whitefield was preaching out-of-doors in several of the commons in London. She decided to go to one of his services in Kennington Common and discovered that John Wesley was there as well (Whitefield preached and Wesley led a hymn). Sarah was again affected by the evangelical message, and the experience prompted her to study Scripture.

At this period in her life, she likened herself to an unbeliever, destined for hell, who "had a real desire to flee from the wrath to come." As much as she tried to have faith she could not, until one day while at home a feeling of peace came over her, and she was then able to believe in Christ, sense God's love for her, and resist things that previously had enticed her.

In spite of this dramatic experience, she still did not claim her sins were forgiven because she did not yet feel the assurance of the Holy Spirit. In 1740, when Wesley established his London headquarters at the Foundery, Sarah became a member of the society and was constantly there as she sought "a clear sense of the pardoning love of God."

She finally perceived that divine love during a Sunday evening service at the Foundery. Wesley's sermon was based on Ezekiel 37:1–14, and at first Sarah identified with the valley of dry bones. Then, as he read verses 12–14, a change of perspective took place, which she described in a letter to Wesley: ". . . my soul was brought out of the grave of sin, and my feet set upon the Rock of Eternal Ages. Now I could say, Thou art my Lord and my God . . . O what love had I now in my soul! I could have laid down my life for the worst sinner out of hell. I went home to my house justified. I was now exceeding happy."[45]

Grace Sanctifies Thomas Taylor

Thomas Taylor was twenty-three years old when Wesley invited him to attend the 1762 Methodist Conference. Taylor was a Calvinist Methodist preacher, and he did not subscribe to Wesley's teaching that there was an Altogether stage of salvation. In spite of this doctrinal difference, Taylor went

45. "Sarah Clay," *AM* 6:528–31, 582–85.

to the conference and anticipated spending the following year in London with Wesley learning Methodist doctrine and discipline. To his surprise, he was offered an appointment to preach in Wales, which he accepted.

His original plan abandoned, he instead began an independent study of Methodist doctrine, especially its teachings on sanctification. As a result of praying, studying Scripture, and reading several books on the subject, including Wesley's *A Plain Account of Christian Perfection*, Taylor came to share the Methodist expectation that, by grace through faith, the image of God could be renewed and a Christian could inwardly and outwardly imitate Christ.

Approximately twenty years after joining the Methodists, he published an account of his experience in the *Arminian Magazine* and explained that, while he had not reached the Altogether stage, there were moments when he was conscious that the primary motivation of his behaviors was love. He wrote: "I prayed that the will of God might be done in me as it is done in heaven; that God would create in my soul his whole image, and root out every root of bitterness, unto the coming of our Lord Jesus Christ . . . I might refer to several declarations of St. Paul, such as Gal. ii. 20. c. vi. 14. Phil. iii. 8. c. xv. 20 [*sic*]. All which imply the same thing. Now all these texts speak of a state which I have not attained; but I follow on towards it. And I have no doubt but he will make a full end of sin, and bring in everlasting righteousness."[46]

Grace Perfects Elizabeth Harper

In his introduction to Elizabeth Harper's journal, Wesley explained that her experience exemplified the character traits he associated with the Altogether stage. The infirmities, temptations, uncertainties, and sinful impulses from which Elizabeth prayed to be set free are consistent with Wesley's definition of Christian perfection, as are the inward and outward examples of holiness she exhibited.[47]

Fear of death brought the twenty-nine-year-old Elizabeth to the Methodist society in Redruth, Cornwall, and she experienced justification by faith and assurance of pardon several months later, on Easter Sunday

46. "Thomas Taylor," and "A supplement," *AM* 3:382 and 4:587–89.

47. Harper, *An Extract*. Compare to Sermon 40, "Christian Perfection," and "Earnest Appeal," §55, *Works* 2:103–19; 11:66, 67.

1764, while receiving communion at her church.[48] She prayed for faith to believe in holiness of heart and life, a prayer that she claimed was answered in 1765.

The journal extract does not pinpoint a specific date when this change occurred; however, at some point during the last week of August, she went from reacting in anger when provoked to turning to God in prayer whenever she felt angry or harried. The journal entries for that week begin with mention of her prayers for faith to believe in the promise of full salvation. Later that same week the entry for Friday reads, "How shall I praise the Lord, for what he has done for my Soul? O the Love of a dear Redeemer to sinful Dust and Ashes! Praise the Lord, O my Soul, and all that is within me praise his Holy Name."[49] The next week (and every month after that until her death in 1768), the journal entries report instances when God enabled her to resist the temptation to sin.

Typically, the temptations mentioned in the journal consist of inattentiveness during church or private prayers, impatience with household members and while working in her husband's shop, and disputes over religious matters (with others or with herself). She handled each temptation by immediately turning to God in prayer and imploring God to help her resist the impulse to sin.[50]

The marks of inward holiness recorded in Harper's journal include a sense of dependence upon God, a calm acceptance of God's will, a desire to grow in righteousness, a concern for the temporal and spiritual well-being of others, an ability to overcome sinful affections and replace them with holy ones, and a sense of the presence of God.[51] There are multiple references to occasions when Harper prayed for evidence that she had reached the Altogether stage, petitioned God for an increase in faith so that her evidence might be clearer, and gave thanks when her prayers were answered and her perception of God's grace was brightened.[52] The satisfaction she derived from participating in religious conversations and from performing

48. Harper, *An Extract*, vii.

49. Ibid., 12, 13.

50. See examples at *Harper*, journal entries 7 September, 4 October, 2 November, and 22 December 1765.

51. See examples at *Harper*, journal entries 19 October 1765, 23 December 1765, 6 May 1766, 18 June 1766, 5 December 1766, and 10 November 1767.

52. *Harper*, 12 August, 15 August, 28 August, 17 September, 21 September, 20 November 1765, 9 February, 10 February, 10 March, and 1 December 1766.

works of mercy are consistent with the signs of outward holiness as described in Wesley's writings.[53]

Grace Glorifies Katherine Murray

Stories of holy deaths are another example of the type of religious testimonials Wesley published. Such reports were intended to inspire and motivate readers to seek a personal experience of the power of religion on this side of heaven.[54]

The story of Katherine Murray's death is an example of the Methodist holy dying genre, and it repeats many of the elements found in other Methodist biographies. Similar to William Ferguson, Katherine (from the town of Carrick-on-Suir in Ireland) revered God until she became a teenager. Like John Pawson, her first reaction to the Methodists was negative. Only after their message convicted her of sin did she join the Methodist society. She prayed for faith for several months before finally receiving a sense of the love of God, as had Sarah Crosby. She and Elizabeth Harper both struggled to resist temptation (and sometimes succumbed) even after reaching the Altogether stage.

Katherine was in poor health for four years before her death at the age of thirty-eight. On the day she died, she is reported to have said, "Oh! You can't conceive the joy I feel. You know but in part, but when that which is perfect is come, you shall know even as you are known . . . Glory to Jesus! O love Jesus! Love Jesus! He is a glorious Jesus! He has now made me fit for himself. When the harvest is ripe, the sickle is put in."[55]

All six Methodist accounts follow Wesley's order of salvation—repentance, faith, holiness, heaven. Though the reports come from different regions of the British Isles and represent both men and women, preachers and laity, there is no difference in their description of the stages of salvation. The

53. See examples at *Harper*, journal entries 3 February 1767 and 23 January 1768. Religious conversation as a mark of holiness is mentioned in Sermon 23 and "Earnest Appeal," §55, *Works* 1:517 and 11:67.

54. *AM* 4:153; Wesley to Miss March, 5 July 1768, and Wesley to Mary Bosanquet, 28 December 1768, *Letters*.

55. Journal entry, 21 July 1767, *Works* 22:91–95.

terminology they used to describe their encounters with the power of religion and the transformational impact that experience had upon their souls is consistent with the descriptions of the faith experience that are found in Wesley's publications.

The testimonials also exhibit a shared conviction that individuals can accurately discern their spiritual state. All six knew beyond a doubt that they were once unrepentant sinners. With certainty, they knew the moment when they trusted in Christ for salvation. They were convinced that they knew when the process of sanctification began and made them a new creation.

Exceptional Methodists

There were exceptions to the rule of certainty, however. Occasionally, Wesley encountered Methodists whose outward behaviors reflected the Altogether stage but whose faith experience deviated from the normal Methodist pattern. Wesley offered a variety of explanations to account for these differences.

He argued that in some cases physical ailments, especially nervous disorders, interfered with the ability of the spiritual senses to perceive the witness of the Holy Spirit because the faculties of the soul depended upon the health of the body, especially the brain. Methodists suffering from psychological illnesses, for example, might fear that they were stuck at the Almost stage because they never felt assurance of forgiveness or sensed God's love even after they had been justified. Whenever he suspected that a psychological disorder was the cause of a person's spiritual unease, Wesley reassured them they had been saved by faith even when the brain could not register that the new birth had indeed taken place.[56]

A person's temperament might also affect the spiritual senses. At least that was the explanation Wesley gave for his own lack of spiritual perception. His knowledge of things not seen was based primarily on Scripture and reason, he told one correspondent, and was hardly ever based on impressions or a direct testimony of the Spirit. He did not claim to have a sense of the invisible and eternal worlds or even a sustained sense of assurance after his Aldersgate experience. Consequently, though he encouraged Methodists to pursue the goal of holiness, happiness, and certainty,

56. Sermon 77, III.6, and "Letter to Rutherforth," I.4, *Works* 3:100, 9:376.

he never pronounced himself an Altogether Christian. The calm, reasonable disposition that made him an effective organizer of the Revival also seemed to hinder him from experiencing the power of religion as did other Methodists.[57]

Wesley's theory of the spiritual senses suggests that another type of religious experience, one that did not pass through all the stages of the order of salvation, was possible. Wesley taught that the spiritual senses were opened at the moment of justification, and given the Anglican position on infant baptism, this would imply that the spiritual senses of infants are opened when they are baptized. Theoretically, if those justified as infants unfailingly respond to God's grace and have faith in Christ, and if their bodies stay healthy and they have the right temperament, then they might spend their lives transitioning between the Awake, Abiding, and Altogether stages and never experience the Asleep or Almost stage. On the contrary, they would always sense God's love for them and feel assured that they were the children of God.[58]

Such cases were rare because most people, in Wesley's opinion, succumb to the "desire of the flesh, the desire of the eyes, and the pride of life." These physical, aesthetic, and social impulses are not harmful in and of themselves; however, if they become temptations that are overindulged, then they can mutate into the outward sins of gluttony, materialism, and self-aggrandizing. If temptation turned into sin, then it would cause the spiritual senses to close, and worldly judgments, desires, designs, conversations, and actions would dominate the soul rather than the power of God's grace. (Wesley once wrote that he sinned away the justifying grace he received at his baptism by the time he was ten.)[59]

To protect his followers from the degenerating effect that sin had on the spiritual senses and the functions of the soul, Wesley continually encouraged Methodists to search their inmost souls not only for evidence of

57. Rack, *Reasonable Enthusiast*, 545–50. Five months after his Aldersgate experience, Wesley finally concluded that even though he did not have the Witness of the Spirit, he did have the witness of his own spirit (i.e., his own reasoning ability). He recognized that his judgments, desires, designs, conversations, and actions had been transformed by grace, and he reasoned that these changes were indications that he was a new creature. Journal entry, 14 October 1738, *Works* 19:16–19.

58. This is the implication of statements made in "The Early Conferences," (1744) [§16], *Works* 10:128.

59. Sermon 7, II.2, Sermon 14, "The Repentance of Believers," I.5–7, "Earnest Appeal," par. 50, and Journal entry 24 May 1738, §1; *Works* 1:226 (n. 64), 227, 338–39; 18:242; and *Notes* Jas 4:4 and 1 John 2:16.

holiness, happiness, and certainty, but also for signs that they were straying from the example of Christ and in need of the power that could help them resist temptations. Methodists were disciplined; they worked out their salvation by using the form of religion while they waited to experience the power that could turn them into new creatures. This discipline kept them focused on the goal of the Christian life, and it preserved the vitality of Methodism.

FOUR

Examining Methodist Discipline

From this short sketch of Methodism (so called) any man of understanding may easily discern that it is only plain scriptural religion, guarded by a few prudential regulations. The essence of it is holiness of heart and life; the circumstantials all point to this. And as long as they are joined together in the people called Methodists, no weapon formed against them shall prosper. But if even the circumstantial parts are despised, the essential will soon be lost. And if ever the essential parts should evaporate, what remains will be dung and dross.

—*Thoughts upon Methodism*

THE ESSENCE OF THE Methodist spirit was Christ-likeness. Anyone seeking this stage of salvation was a "brother, and sister, and mother" to the Methodists. In contrast to a spirit of exclusion and suspicion, Wesley promoted a "catholic spirit" that celebrated religious vitality wherever it could be found. This tolerant spirit was extended to members of other denominations who believed in the basic principles of Christianity, that is, those who trusted God, had faith in Christ, loved God and neighbor (including enemies), experienced the spiritual affections of joy, thankfulness, and happiness, had a single intention to glorify God in all activities, lived according to God's moral law, and performed good works. Any Christian who attained this ideal standard reflected the Spirit of "plain scriptural religion," as far as Wesley was concerned.[1] (To encourage this tolerant outlook, reports were

1. Sermon 4, Sermon 23, "Sermon on the Mount, III," IV, Sermon 39, "The Catholic Spirit," I.12–I.18, "The Character of a Methodist," and "Thoughts upon Methodism," §8, *Works* 1:159–80, 530; 2:87–89; 9:32–42, 529; and *Notes* Rom 14:17.

read at Methodist society meetings that described what the power of God's grace was accomplishing in other renewal movements.)[2]

The Methodists were advised that advancing through the stages of salvation and becoming an Altogether Christian required divine initiative and human prudence. Grace convicted and saved the soul and renewed it in the image of God. Methodist discipline guarded that gift and protected the vitality of Wesley's movement as long as Methodist spiritual practices continued to point them towards the goal of the Christian life.

In opposition to the Moravians, who discouraged spiritual disciplines out of concern that people would trust in works rather than in Christ for salvation, Wesley advised the Methodists to use the outward forms of religion while they waited for the power of religion, and he cited Scripture in support of his position. Christians must, like the Israelites, obey God's command and wait to be saved by "'marching forward' with all their might" (Exod 14:13–31). To do this, Christians had to obey Christ's commands and perform works of piety and works of mercy (i.e., give alms, pray, fast, search the Scriptures, engage in holy conversations, and partake of the Lord's Supper) while anticipating the transformation of their souls.[3]

Wesley taught that disciplines such as church or religious society assemblies, stewardship (of the body, the faculties of the soul, and material goods), works of piety, and works of mercy could convey God's grace into the soul. He encouraged the Methodists to practice these outward forms of religion while waiting for God's power to yield the inward fruits of the Spirit, especially love of God and neighbor.[4] His religious advice can be diagrammatically represented by a target chart where the bull's eye denotes love and the inner ring signifies the other fruits of the Spirit produced by grace through faith, while the outer rings correspond to the various forms of religion.

2. "A Plain Account of the People called Methodist," *Works* 9:266.

3. Sermon 16, III, IV.5, Sermon 27, §4, Sermon 98, §1, and Journal entry, 23–29 June 1740, *Works* 1:384–92, 594; 3:385; 19:155–59. See Christ's commands in Matt 6:1–18; 7:7–11; 26:26–29; John 5:39.

4. Sermon 92, "On Zeal," II.5, and "Large" *Minutes* (1763), [§40.1–7], *Works* 3:313; 10:855–58. Wesley's argument in Sermon 92 builds on the advice of James Garden. See Maddox, "Wesley's Prescription for Making Disciples of Jesus Christ," n. 44.

The Form and Power of Religion

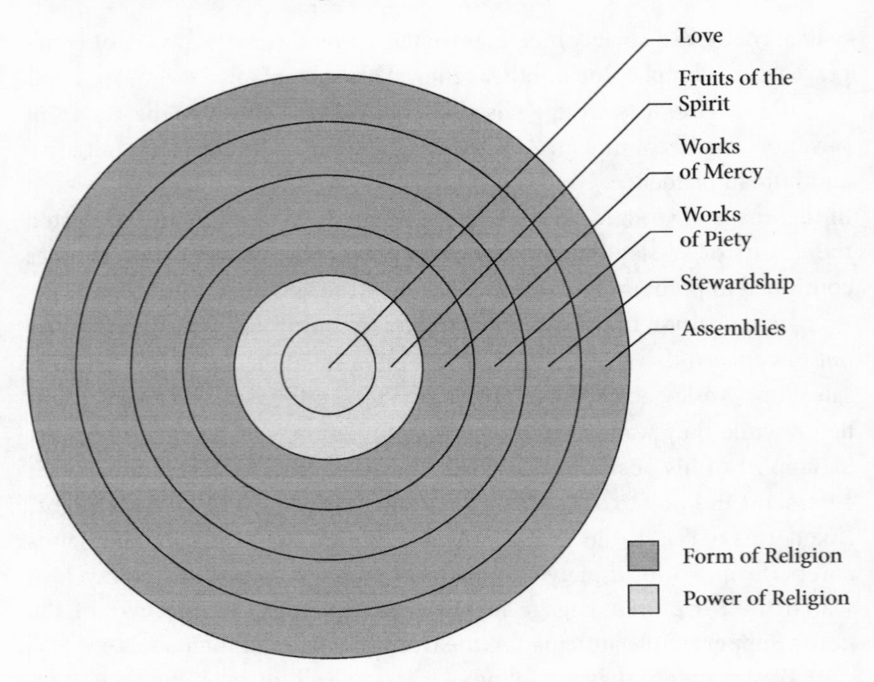

A series of cylinders can be used to diagram the relationship between the form and power of religion in Wesley's order of salvation. The first cylinder represents Wesley's teaching that outward forms of religion can serve as channels of preventing and convincing grace for the Asleep and the Almost. The cylinder is hollow at its core, indicating that the power of religion is not present at these stages.

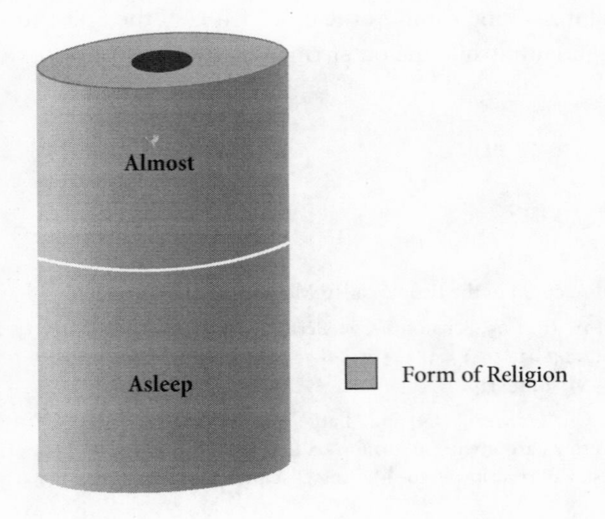

Holiness of heart and life, happiness even in the midst of trials, and the certainty of faith were all indicators that an interior renewal had taken place in the soul. These new creatures had experienced the power of religion and were at the Awake, Abiding, or Altogether stage of salvation.

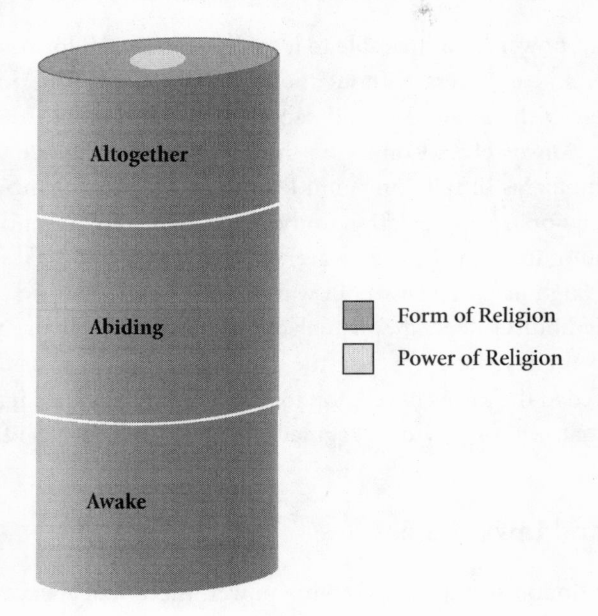

Even after the Awake receive the gift of faith and experience the power of religion, they still need the power of God's grace communicated by the forms of religion if they are to advance through the Abiding to the Altogether stage of salvation. The inner core of the Awake-Abiding-Altogether cylinder is no longer hollow, representing that both the form and the power of religion are present at these stages.

To explain the relationship between the form and the power of religion, Wesley would occasionally quote the maxim "The soul and the body make a man; the spirit and discipline make a Christian." The saying comes from *Devotions in the Ancient Way of Offices*, an Anglican revision of a book of prayers by the seventeen-century Catholic writer John Austin. The quotation is part of a prayer for Friday Matins, which requests divine assistance to maintain a balance between the outward performance of disciplines and the inward pursuit of holiness, happiness, and certainty:

> MY God! never let me rely upon any outward performances, so as to neglect the improvement of my mind; lest my fasting become an

> unprofitable trouble, and my prayer a vain lip-labor. The soul and the body make a man, and the spirit and discipline make a Christian. Never let me so pretend to inward perfection, as to slight the outward observances of religion; lest my thoughts grow proud and fantastic, and all my arguments but a cover for licentiousness.[5]

Form without power is comparable to a soulless body; the forms are dead, unprofitable, and pointless without the desire to receive the power that alone can renew the *imago Dei* and can cause advancement in the stages of salvation. Conversely, a fixation on the power of God's grace to the exclusion of the forms of religion could lead to spiritual arrogance and duplicitous behavior. An appreciation for both the form and power of religion promoted humility (that is, the awareness that growth in grace was not achieved through personal effort but was initiated and sustained by God).

The Methodists needed spiritual disciplines to instill the power of religion into their souls and cause the growth of the fruits of the Spirit. They also needed the forms of religion to keep them vigilant against natural tendencies that, without prudent regulation, could cause backsliding.[6]

Outward and Inward Sins

Without continuous infusions of divine power, there was always a chance that thoughts, behaviors, and actions that were harmful to the soul and the spiritual senses would proliferate and spiritual vitality would wane. This degeneration could happen quickly or slowly, Wesley warned; the rate of decline depended on the type of sin involved. Sins of commission, or outward sins (defined as knowingly breaking God's moral law), instantly closed the spiritual senses. Sins of omission, or "negative inward sin" (such as ignoring God's call to service, neglecting to pray for discernment, and failing to pursue holiness because of spiritual sloth), initiated a slow slide backwards into the Almost or, worse, the Asleep stage of salvation. Omissions could lead to "positive inward sin" (unholy affections that are left unchecked) that also caused the spiritual senses to shut down and faith to be lost.[7]

5. *Library* 42:199; compare to Austin, *Devotions in the Ancient Way of Offices*, 245–46. "Spirit and discipline" quote also in Sermon 113, "The Late Work of God in North America," I.7, Sermon 122, "Causes of the Inefficacy of Christianity," §7, and Journal entry 17 August 1750, *Works* 3:598; 4:90; 20:357; and Wesley to William Church, 13 October 1778, and Wesley to Adam Clarke, 3 January 1787, *Letters*.

6. Sermon 16, I.1, II.1, and Sermon 27, III.2, *Works* 1:378, 381, 605.

7. Sermon 19, Sermon 46, "The Wilderness State," Sermon 48, "Self-Denial," and

Foregoing private prayer was for Wesley the most obvious sin of omission. He warned, "Nothing can be more plain than that the life of God in the soul does not continue, much less increase, unless we use all opportunities of communing with God, and pouring out our hearts before him . . . And if we long or frequently intermit [these secret exercises of the soul], [that life] will gradually die away."[8]

Neglecting to reprove one's neighbor was another sin of omission that Wesley cautioned against. When Methodists observed someone committing a sin, Wesley taught them to gently explain to the sinner that such conduct damaged and endangered the soul.[9]

Avoiding this type of face-to-face confrontation allowed feelings of indignation to fester, Wesley warned—feelings that would then degenerate into the inward sins of pride, anger, and resentment. These emotions almost always lead to the outward sin of evil-speaking. Wesley characterized this behavior as a sin of commission because it broke the moral law stated in Titus 3:2, "Speak evil of no one." Practically every conversation contained some element of backbiting or tale-bearing, Wesley pointed out, which meant that the Methodists had to be especially vigilant to escape committing this sin.[10]

Maintaining their vigilance against sins of commission and omission and sustaining their spiritual vitality was possible, Wesley advised the Methodists, if they remained disciplined. To help the Methodists properly use the form of religion while waiting for the power of religion, Wesley experimented with an organization-wide disciplinary system, adding to and revising it throughout his ministry, always searching for the method that would protect Methodists from backsliding and encourage them to seek

---

Journal entry 6 May 1785, *Works* 1:439–40; 2:208, 210–11, 246–48; 23:355; *Notes* Eph 6:18 and Heb 12:14; and *Letters* 11 and 14 December 1773.

8. Sermon 46, II.4, *Works* 2: 209.

9. Ibid., II.5, 209–10.

10. Sermon 49, "The Cure of Evil-Speaking," Sermon 75, II.13, 14, *Works* 2:253; 3:65. Also mentioned in "Advice to the People called Methodists," §10, *Works* 9:126. Matthew 18:15–17 provided the rule that Wesley followed in order to avoid this sin. First, meekly and lovingly confront the sinner after praying for guidance. Second, if the rebuke is rebuffed, then take along one or two Altogether Christians to the next meeting with the sinner. Third, if the sinner is still unrepentant, then notify the leader of the church or society. Fourth, if reconciliation is not achieved, then continue to extend common courtesy to the sinner, but end the relationship, and never speak about the sinner again except in prayer. Sermon 49, *Works* 2:257–62.

the Altogether stage. This system built on the spiritual practices that he had followed at Oxford and in Georgia.

Resolutions and Examinations

Wesley developed a discipline of resolution-making and self-examining while he was at Oxford. Motivated by his reading of the religious advice book *Holy Living and Dying*, Wesley resolved to "redeem the time" and monitor how he spent his days. To aid in this task, he began keeping a diary in 1725, and he maintained that habit for the rest of his life. The diaries are a record of his daily activities, which typically began with 4:00 a.m. private prayers and ended at his 9:30 p.m. bedtime. The amount of detail recorded in the diaries varies over the years, but the basic intention—to keep track of his attempt to glorify God in every aspect of his life—remains the same.[11]

The first resolution recorded in the diary that Wesley started in 1725 reads, "A General Rule in All Actions, Whenever you do an action, consider how Christ did or would do the like, and do you imitate his example." Over the years this simple statement of his intention to imitate Christ would evolve into a list of approximately twenty questions that he used to guide his daily self-examinations while he was at Oxford. By reading over his diary record and reflecting on such questions as, "Have I frequent Thought of God and Ejaculations to Him? Do I maintain Warm, Even Purpose of obeying him? Am I active and zealous in doing what Good I can?" Wesley could examine his behaviors and activities for signs of sinful tendencies and influences, repent of any transgression of his resolution to follow the example of Christ, and renew his commitment to regulate his emotional and social life by the standard of holiness.[12]

The diaries of Charles Wesley, Benjamin Ingham, and George Whitefield contain self-examination questions that are almost identical to those in John's diaries. Entries in their diaries indicate on which days of the week and at what time during the day these four friends engaged in self-examination, evidence that this spiritual discipline was a common practice among the Methodists at Oxford.[13] At some of their meetings, the Oxford

11. Ward and Heitzenrater, "Editorial Introduction," *Works* 18:304–6.

12. Heitzenrater, "Oxford Methodists," 59, 60, 132.

13. Ingham, *Diary of an Oxford Methodist*, 19 n. 31.

Methodists would share their diaries and reveal to their friends how they were faring in their search for the power of religion.[14]

The article, "A Scheme of Self-examination used by the first Methodists in Oxford" provides a clue to the type of resolution-making and daily review that Wesley encouraged his friends to practice. Only questions for Sunday (on love of God) and Monday (on love of neighbor) are listed, though in another publication Wesley referred to the list as a "scheme of daily self-examination."[15]

To promote their resolve to love God, the Oxford Methodists were supposed to reflect on the intentions that had motivated all of their words and actions over the course of the day so that they could determine if those intentions had been solely focused on doing God's will. The resolution to pray every day was also supposed to inspire their love of God, and the *Scheme* catalogued different methods of prayer (private, public, ejaculatory, meditation, etc.) and asked whether or not they had been used.

When examining themselves for evidence of love of neighbor, the early Methodists were to review the day for instances when they had done all the good they could, engaged in holy conversations, exhibited holy affections, evangelized other students and strangers, and offered prayers of intercession.

In addition to sharing his resolutions and self-examination questions with the Oxford Methodists, Wesley also wrote out a scheme of discipline for the pupils he tutored. This guide to the making and keeping of resolutions formed the basis of his first publication, *Collection of Forms of Prayer* (1733). Even after his Aldersgate conversion, Wesley continued to publish and sell this collection of virtue-based prayers and examination questions (the last edition to come out during his lifetime was published in 1788).

The questions in the *Collection* required readers to search their hearts and lives for evidence of holiness. (Were their thoughts constantly focused on God? Did they have holy or unholy affections? Did they have a single intention to obey God? Were their conversations holy?) Other questions asked if they had followed the form of religion—do no harm (had they harmed others by speaking evil of them?), do good (had they done all the good they could?), use the means of grace (had they prayed that morning?).

14. Ibid., 4, 17.

15. Wesley, "A Scheme of Self-Examination," *Works* (Jackson) 11:521–23; and Sermon 79, "On Dissipation," §20, *Works* 3:124.

These questions were to be reviewed every night, while other questions were only to be used on specific days of the week.[16]

The resolution to become virtuous was also emphasized in the *Collection*. A different virtue was to be reflected on each day. Sunday's questions focused on love of God; Monday's on love of neighbor; Tuesday's on humility; Wednesday's on mortification; Thursday's on resignation and meekness; the directions for Friday required the examiner to go back to Wednesday's questions on mortification; and Saturday's questions were about thankfulness.

The *Collection*'s daily morning and evening prayers also reflect the virtue assigned for that day. Sunday's prayers reflect on the duty to love God. Monday's prayers express the desire to imitate God by extending loving-kindness to everyone. Tuesday includes the petition to make humility the ruling habit of the soul. Wednesday's prayer is a confession of sin. Thursday's supplication is to always do the will of God. Friday meditates upon the sufferings of Christ. Saturday's expresses gratitude for God's goodness and mercy.[17]

These directions for engaging in virtue-based prayer and self-examination are consistent with the religious advice books Wesley was reading at this time. The idea of focusing on a different virtue each day of the week can be found in Robert Nelson's *The Practice of True Devotion*. Nelson argued that this resolution was necessary because practicing virtue was the only way to attain Christian perfection. The writings of William Law, Richard Allestree, and John Norris all agree with the premise that the development of Christian virtues is the means to advance to the Altogether stage.[18]

While in Georgia, Wesley adapted his method of resolution-making and self-examination to a group setting. His diary indicates that 185 religious society meetings were held in Savannah and thirty-six meetings in Frederica during his nine-month tenure. The members of these small groups resolved to observe the forms of religion and to engage in means of grace at their meetings. Their group practices included hymn singing, the reading of devotional literature, the discussion of religious subjects, exhortation to pursue inward and outward holiness, and the reproving of sin.[19]

16. Heitzenrater, "Oxford Methodists," 133, 245–46.

17. Wesley, "Collection of forms of prayer," *Works* (Jackson) 11:203–37.

18. Nelson, *True Devotion*, 67–76; Law, *Serious Call*, 33; Allestree, *Decay of Christian Piety*, 17–21; Norris, *Treatise concerning Humility*, 185–86.

19. Hammond, "Restoring Primitive Christianity," 198–209.

The practice of candidly discussing their struggles against sinful temptations raised the suspicions of some not in one of Wesley's small groups. Wesley was accused of introducing "Jesuitical Arts" into the colony, and his religious societies were attacked in print:

> Families were divided in Parties; Spies were engaged in many Houses, and the Servants of others bribed and decoyed to let him into all the Secrets of the Families they belonged to; nay, those who had given themselves up to his Spiritual Guidance (more especially Women) were obliged to discover to him their most secret Actions, nay even their Thoughts and the Subject of their Dreams.[20]

A kernel of truth can be found in this outrageous speculation. The primary purpose of Wesley's Saturday evening society was to prepare members for the next day's celebration of the Lord's Supper. Confession of sin was one of the methods of communion preparation outlined by religious advice books such as Allestree's *The Whole Duty of Man*, and *The Worthy Communicant Prepared*, written by John's father. (Allestree and Wesley Sr. suggested that the Ten Commandments could be used as a framework for examination and repentance prior to participating in the Eucharist.) However, the act of repentance discussed in these books was a private undertaking, not a group project.

In spite of the suspicions raised by outsiders, Wesley continued organizing and leading confessional societies. He played a part in starting the Fetter Lane Society in London soon after his return from Georgia. Following a Moravian practice, the members of the society were divided into Bands—eight small groups for men and two for women—which met weekly "to confess their faults one to another and to pray for one another that they may be healed" (Jas 5:16).[21]

The next year his old Oxford Methodist friend, George Whitefield, wrote him in March 1739 requesting John's help with the large numbers of Christians who had been awakened by Whitefield's field preaching in and around Bristol: "Many are ripe for bands. I leave that entirely to you—I am but a novice; you are acquainted with the great things of God."[22] Wesley

20. Tailfer, *True and Historical Narrative of the Colony of Georgia*, 42.

21. Davies, "Introduction," *Works* 9:7–9; Rack, *Reasonable Enthusiast*, 187; and Heitzenrater, *Wesley*, 79.

22. Letter, 22 March 1739, *Works* 25:612.

complied with this request and by July had founded a Methodist society in Bristol with accompanying bands.[23]

Thus began a pattern that would eventually develop into the standard evangelism technique of the Methodist revival. Whenever Wesley entered a new community, he preached in the open air in order to reach those at the Asleep stage.[24] If possible, he would also try to preach to the Almost Christians in the churches and in the non-Methodist religious societies. The people who were convinced of sin or spiritual lethargy by his message were organized into Methodist societies. Society meetings would then be held on a regular basis, and in his absence, lay preachers would lead these services of prayer, singing, testifying, and exhortation. Bands of between five and ten members were also established within the society, some for the Abiding, who were actively waiting to be made Altogether Christians, and others for backsliders seeking forgiveness.[25]

In 1741, a new element was added to Wesley's disciplinary system. Starting with the Methodist societies in Bristol, Wesley began what would become the regular practice of interviewing every member of the societies four times a year at a quarterly meeting. At these meetings members vouched for each other's conduct or in some cases accused one another of misconduct. Members had the right to face their accusers and defend themselves or confess their faults. Wesley gave tickets to those who were still in good standing with the society after his examination, which functioned as an admission ticket to society meetings.[26]

The class meeting is another revision to Wesley's system for group examinations, and it is the only branch of Methodist discipline mentioned in "Thoughts upon Methodism." The first Methodist classes were organized in 1742 as part of a fundraising effort, not as a form of spiritual discipline. In order to pay off the debt on the Methodist preaching house in Bristol, the suggestion was made that every member should contribute a penny a week to the cause. Accordingly, the society was divided into classes of twelve members each, and class leaders were assigned the task of collecting the twelve-cent offering and making up the difference out of their own pocket if any member was unable to donate a penny that week.[27]

23. Davies, "Introduction," *Works* 9:10.

24. "Large" *Minutes (1753)*, [§9] *Works* 10:846.

25. Davies, "An Introductory Comment," *Works* 9:67; and Heitzenrater, *Wesley*, 104.

26. Heitzenrater, *Wesley*, 123; and Davies, "Introduction," *Works* 9:19, 20.

27. "Thoughts," §5, and Journal entry, 15 February 1742, *Works* 9:528; 19:251.

The formation of classes led to an unintended consequence. Occasionally, when a class leader stopped by members' homes or places of employment to collect their offerings, the leader caught the members engaging in sinful behavior (e.g., inebriated, swearing, or fighting with their spouses). These incidents were reported to Wesley, who realized that the class leaders could strengthen a weakness in the Methodist support system.

As he made the rounds of the Methodist societies and conducted examinations, Wesley observed that society members who were not in a band sometimes lost their motivation to work towards the higher stages of salvation and began to fall back Asleep.[28] Perhaps the class leader could intervene and prevent this loss of faith, Wesley reasoned. By observing members' conduct beyond the structured environment of a religious service or a quarterly conference, the class leaders' perception of backsliding among the class members was keener than that of the preachers. When the leaders discovered someone teetering on the edge between the Almost and the Asleep stage, they could instantly correct and steady the member. Furthermore, if the intervention proved unsuccessful, then the membership of the unrepentant Methodist could be revoked before that behavior harmed the faith or the reputation of the other society members.[29]

Wesley directed the class leaders to ask members about the state of their souls, to encourage anyone who was struggling to live a holy life, and to rebuke anyone who had ceased to make the effort. The leaders soon reported that it was not always possible to carry on these intensely personal conversations in the members' homes and businesses. As a result, another variation on the task of the class leader was made. Instead of individual meetings, a group meeting was proposed. All the members of a class came together, reported on their search for the power of godliness, and confronted members who were known to be struggling yet were unwilling to confess their faults.[30]

Classes were soon organized in Methodist societies throughout England, and in 1743 Wesley published a job description that detailed how the class leaders were to perform their new function as spiritual guide. The class leader's main task was the weekly examination of all the members of the class to gauge their state of spiritual health, and to offer them advice on how to persevere towards the Altogether stage. (The class leaders also

28. "Plain Account of the Methodists," I.9, *Works* 9:257–58.

29. Ibid., II.1–4, and "Thoughts," §6, *Works* 9:260–61, 528–29.

30. "Plain Account of the Methodists," II.6, *Works* 9:261–62.

collected whatever the members wished to donate to help cover the expenses of the society, and each week they were to meet with the assistants and stewards that Wesley had appointed to the society in order to share the results of the class examination and to turn in the donation.)[31]

The 1743 publication for class leaders included resolutions that all society members were to follow. The class leaders were to evaluate each member according to the general rules: do no harm, do good, use the means of grace. Instructions for the band leaders were added in 1744, and these rules stipulated that in addition to questions about the general rules resolution, members were to be asked if they had committed any sins or faced any temptations since the last meeting.[32]

In 1753 another method of group examination was added to Methodist discipline to help ensure that members were living up to their resolutions. At the annual meeting between Wesley and his assistants, it was agreed that the assistants could help Wesley with his pastoral care obligations by examining and instructing members in their homes.[33]

The Methodist disciplinary system underwent yet another revision ten years later. At the 1763 Conference, Wesley stated his dissatisfaction with the assistants' handling of home visitations. To help them with this task, he listed some sample questions in the Conference *Minutes* that could be used when the assistants examined members in their homes: "Have you Family Prayer? Do you read the Scripture in your Family? Have you a fixed Time for private Prayer?"[34]

These guidelines did not improve the situation to Wesley's satisfaction by the time of the 1766 Conference. Wesley complained that most Methodists had only a superficial religion and did not understand the basic principles of Methodist doctrine. Plain preaching was not the solution, he counseled. The only way to help Methodists maintain their resolve to imitate Christ was to give them one-on-one home instruction. As he had three years earlier, once again Wesley provided his assistants with a sample examination method in the *Minutes* from the Conference.

The assistants were to test members' knowledge of Methodist doctrine by going to members' homes and asking such question as, "Do you believe

31. "General Rules," *Works* 9:69, 70. A further elaboration of this job description is found in Journal entry 3 April 1771, *Works* 22:267.

32. "Rules of the Band Societies," *Works* 9:77–79.

33. "Large" *Minutes* (1753), [§16.4] *Works* 10:848.

34. "Large" *Minutes* (1763), [§16.5] *Works* 10:848

you have Sin in you? That you was born in Sin? What does sin deserve? What remedy has God provided for guilty, helpless Sinners?" Wesley also suggested phrasing the answer as a question: "What is Repentance? Sorrow for Sin, or a Conviction that we are guilty, helpless Sinners? What is Faith? A divine Conviction of things not seen?"[35] Wesley found that follow-up questions were sometimes necessary:

> "How do you think your many and great Sins will be pardoned?" They answer, "By repenting and mending my Life," and never mention Christ. I ask farther, "But do you think your Amendment will make satisfaction for your past Sins?" They will answer, "We hope so, or else we know not what will." . . . Ask them farther, "Can you be saved without the Death of Christ?" They immediately say, "No." And if you ask, "What has he done or suffered for you?" They will say, "He shed his Blood for us," and profess, they trust in That for Salvation.[36]

After examining members' understanding of the doctrines of repentance and justification, the assistants were next to ask about the member's stage of salvation. At the very least, Wesley wanted each member to be at the Almost stage and to resolve to seek the Altogether stage by forsaking inward and outward sin, seeking holy companions, and using the Means of Grace.[37]

At the end of the interview, the head of the household was to be assigned the task of examining the children's and servants' answers to Wesley's catechism, *Instructions for Children*, every Sunday evening before bedtime.[38] (Advice for heads of families could also be found in Wesley's sermon "On Family Religion," which emphasized the importance of restraining family members from committing outward sins and regularly instructing them in Methodist doctrines.)[39]

The 1780 Conference *Minutes* added a new emphasis to the home visit task, which specified that all of the preachers were expected to engage in these one-on-one conversations: "Every traveling Preacher must instruct [members] from house to house."[40]

35. Annual *Minutes* (1766) [§29(4)], *Works* 10:337.
36. Annual *Minutes* (1766) [§29(5)], *Works* 10:337–38.
37. Annual *Minutes* (1766) [§29(8–10)], *Works* 10:338.
38. Annual *Minutes* (1766) [§29(11)], *Works* 10:339.
39. Sermon 94, III.1, III.5, *Works* 3:338–40.
40. "Large" *Minutes* (1780) [§13.1], *Works* 10:912.

The practice of home examination impacted the procedures followed by Methodist classes and bands. A new emphasis on Methodist doctrine can be seen in the *Arminian Magazine* article "Of the right Method of Meeting Classes and Bands in Methodist-Societies," published in 1781. The article directs class leaders to instruct class members on the "first principles of religion" and to explain to them the meaning of their preacher's sermons, in addition to inquiring about the state of a person's soul. The band leaders were not only to ask members about their resolve to progress towards the Altogether stage, but they were also to test members on their understanding of holiness.[41]

The assistants were also subjected to an examination of their understanding of Methodist doctrine. Wesley told the assistants that they should think of themselves as "Learners, rather than Teachers: As young Students at the University: For whom therefore a Method of Study is expedient in the highest Degree." Many of the religious advice books and texts on doctrine and church history that Wesley proceeded to assign to his assistants were ones that he had required his pupils to read when he was a university tutor. This reading schedule became part of the 1747 examination questions posed to the assistants in addition to questions about their observation of the form of religion:

> Do you rise at 4? Do you study in the method laid down at the last Conference? Do you read the books we advise and no other? Do you see the necessity of regularity in study? What are your chief temptations to irregularity? Do you punctually observe the evening hour of retirement? Are you exact in writing your journal? Do you fast on Friday? Do you converse seriously, usefully and closely? Do you pray before, and have you a determinate end in, every conversation?[42]

In 1751, Charles was given the task of evaluating each of the preachers. To accomplish this assignment, Charles traveled the circuits, listened to the preaching, met with the society members, and dismissed anyone whose sermons were not consistent with Methodist doctrine and whose conduct did not reflect the Methodist spirit.[43]

41. Perronet, *AM* 4:604–6.

42. The Early Conferences, (1746) [§§53, 54] and (1747) [§67], *Works* 10:179–80, 206–7.

43. Charles Wesley, 28 June 1751, *Journal* 2:84. Heitzenrater, *Wesley*, 182–84.

Questions that evaluated the preachers for evidence of inward holiness were added to the 1753 *Minutes* ("Do you walk close with God? Have you now Fellowship with the Father and the Son?"), and questions on the use and enforcement of the forms of religion were added in 1763. The 1763 examination questions for Wesley's assistants remained the standard for the *Minutes* of 1770, 1772, 1780, and 1789, even after some of his "pupils" complained that they were ready to graduate.[44]

The *Minutes* from the 1766 Conference contain a long defense of Wesley's authority over the members of the Methodist societies, including his power to dismiss preachers. To the charges of "shackling free-born Englishmen" and making himself a pope, Wesley responded that the preachers were not enslaved; they were free to quit at any time; and they were under no threat of excommunication if they did choose to leave the Methodists, as Wesley's societies were not churches. Possibly the preachers might gain voting rights at conference after his death, but he discerned that God had given him the burden of determining the membership standards and expectations for all Methodists, and he could not cast off the responsibility as long as he was able to fulfill this divinely appointed duty.[45]

The Final Exam

The various forms of examination that Wesley took upon himself and imposed on others (self-assessment, family reviews, home visitations, band, class and society evaluations, and preacher inspections) encouraged the Methodists in their resolve to pursue the Altogether stage of salvation. By practicing this discipline, the Methodists routinely received communications of grace and prudently regulated injurious inclinations. In addition, resolution-making and forms of examination also helped them anticipate heaven. On Judgment Day, Wesley taught, everyone would be required to give an account of his or her thoughts, words, and actions. By engaging in examinations in this life, the Methodists were preparing for Christ's final examination.

The practice of examination is viewed from an eschatological perspective in the extract of Jeremy Taylor's advice book *Rule and Exercises of Holy Dying* that Wesley published in 1752 as part of the *Christian Library* (a

44. "Large" *Minutes* (1753) [§40], (1763) [§40.1], (1770–1772) [§ 44], and (1780–1789) [§48], *Works* 10:855, 923.

45. Annual *Minutes* (1766) [§29(6)], *Works* 10:329–30.

fifty-volume set of religious advice books edited by Wesley and published between 1749 and 1755): "As therefore every Night we must make our Bed the Memorial of our Grave, so let our Evening Thoughts be an Image of the Day of Judgment."[46]

The next year Wesley published another volume of the *Christian Library* that contained a description of what it will be like on the Last Day when the good steward appears before his Master and gives an accounting of his stewardship. The scene is taken from Matthew Hale's book *Contemplations Moral and Divine*, and it is repeated in Wesley's sermon "The Good Steward." The final exam questions that Christ asks in this sermon are based on Hale's text.[47]

> How didst thou employ thy *soul*?
>
> Didst thou employ thy *understanding* as far as it was capable, according to those directions, namely, in the knowledge of thyself and me?
>
> Didst thou employ thy *memory* according to my will?
>
> Was thy *imagination* employed, not in painting vain images, much less such as nourishing foolish and hurtful desires, but in representing to thee whatever would profit thy soul, and awaken thy pursuit of wisdom and holiness?
>
> Didst thou follow my directions with regard to thy *will*?
>
> Were thy *affections* placed and regulated in such a manner as I appointed in my Word?
>
> Were thy *thoughts* employed according to my will?
>
> How didst thou employ the *body* wherewith I entrusted thee?
>
> How didst thou employ the *worldly goods* which I lodged in thy hands?
>
> Hast thou been a wise and faithful steward with regard to the talents of a mixed nature [i.e., health, strength, popularity, education, authority, time, grace] which I lent thee?

The set of questions regarding the steward's use of grace that culminates the final exam is not found in Hale's version. Instead, these questions reflect Wesley's doctrinal order of salvation. Christ begins the last section of the exam by probing how the steward reacted to the influence of the Holy

46. *Library* 16:159.

47. *Library* 30:101–43. Sermon 51, "The Good Steward," *Works* 2:293–96. Please note, Christ's questions to the Good Steward do not appear in this format in Sermon 51. I streamlined paragraphs III.3–6 to facilitate ease of reading.

Spirit when it attempted to quicken the soul by means of preventing grace (through good desires, enlightening insights, and pricks of conscience). The evaluation moves on to inquire if the steward made the most of the "Spirit of bondage and fear" in the Almost stage. Finally, after receiving the Spirit of adoption and assurance of the forgiveness of sins, Christ asks whether or not the steward sought holiness of heart and life.[48]

Wesley's questioning of every member of the Methodist societies and his insistence that his preachers carry out examinations in every Methodist home should be read against this eschatological backdrop. Ever the tutor, Wesley organized the Methodists into study groups that were prepping for the final oral exam. In a sense they were quizzing one another, reviewing the study guide, and trying to help each other receive a passing grade from the headmaster. Through such discipline they guarded their final salvation.

Progress to the Angelic state was not a forgone conclusion for Wesley. He taught that those who did not work out their salvation and were judged to be unfaithful stewards would be as alienated from God in the next life as they had been in this one.

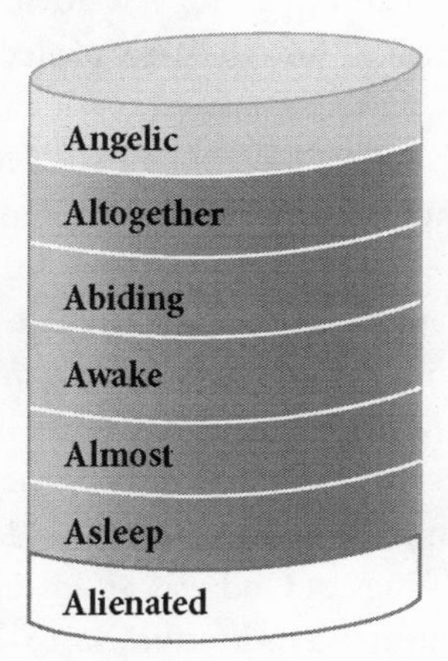

In Wesley's model of salvation, temperament in this life becomes permanent in the next. The habitual inclination of the Asleep to resist God's will and to distance themselves from God's power has eternal consequences. After death, the Alienated experience the pain of their infinite separation from God. The Angelic, in contrast, who made grace their aim while alive,

48. Sermon 51, III.6, *Works* 2:296.

now enjoy an experience of that power that no longer requires the mediation of the form of religion.[49]

The practice of resolving and examining protected the Methodists' sense of present salvation, as well. For Methodism to flourish, Wesley's followers not only had to make resolutions but also to examine their behavior to ensure they were keeping those resolutions. When this discipline of resolving and examining was practiced, the gift of salvation was guarded from sinful impulses. Without it, the Methodists were exposed and spiritually vulnerable because they were less likely to quickly seek God's grace for the power to amend their conduct.

Methodist Backsliding

The greatest temptation to sin Wesley observed besetting the Methodists was the desire to become rich and indulge in a wealthy lifestyle. This was the only threat to Methodist vitality that Wesley spoke against in "Thoughts upon Methodism," and his argument repeats advice that he had frequently given his followers regarding how best to protect themselves from this danger.

Ironically, the more the Methodists pursued holy living, the more the peril posed by riches increased. Righteousness led to frugality and diligence, traits that decreased spending and increased income, which resulted in excess savings. (Wesley taught that any savings beyond the cost for the basic necessities and simple conveniences of life was excessive.)[50]

The love of money was the "principle cause of the decay of true religion in every Christian community," Wesley argued, and it threatened the vitality of Methodism in his day, as well.[51] The desire for worldly things rather than the unseen things of God was an inward sin that was in direct opposition to Christ's command in Matthew 6:19–20, "Do not store up for yourselves treasures on earth, where moth and rust consume and where thieves break in and steal; but store up for yourselves treasures in heaven."

49. Sermon 7, II.1–4; Sermon 15, "The Great Assize," II.12, III.1, Sermon 73, "Of Hell," I.1–4, and Sermon 115, "Dives and Lazarus," I.8, II.7, *Works* 1:225–28, 366–67; 3:34, 35; 4:10, 14, 15; and *Notes* 2 Thess 1:9.

50. Sermon 88, "On Dress," §19, and Sermon 131, "The Danger of Increasing Riches," *Works* 3:256–57; 4:178–86.

51. Sermon 61, "The Mystery of Iniquity," §34, Sermon 87, "The Danger of Riches," §§1–4, and Sermon 108, "On Riches," §§2–4, *Works* 2:468; 3:228–31, 520.

Those who want to become wealthy "fall into temptation, and are trapped by many senseless and harmful desires that plunge people into ruin and destruction" (1 Tim 6:9). In Wesley's reading of this Scripture passage, he emphasized that few seekers of wealth are able to resist the lure of riches; once they have fallen into its snare, inward sin ("every temper that is earthly, sensual, or devilish") commences.[52] When these unholy motivations find an inlet into the soul, the love of God is crowded out and replaced with love of the world, which causes the gradual closing of the spiritual senses.[53]

Wesley's sermons argue that the only way to resist "the desire of the flesh, the desire of the eye, and the pride of life"—impulses that are exacerbated by wealth and degrade the will, affections, and liberty of the soul—is to repent and ground every behavior on the foundation of faith in Christ.[54] Occasionally, the sermons ask pointed questions about this area of Methodist conduct. If Methodists ever found themselves wondering if they were falling into the temptation of desiring riches instead of desiring God, then they only had to reflect on these questions:

> Desire of the Flesh—Are not eating and drinking the greatest pleasures of your life, the most considerable part of your happiness?
>
> Desire of the Eye—Are you not seeking happiness in pretty or elegant apparel, or furniture? Or in new clothes, or books, or in pictures, or gardens?
>
> Pride of Life—Do not *you* seek the praise of men more than the praise of God? Do not *you* lay up, or at least desire and endeavour to lay up, treasures on earth? Are you not then (deal faithfully with your own soul!) more and more alive to the world? And consequently more and more dead to God?[55]

Furthermore, anyone who pursued wealth was actually "serving mammon," Wesley warned, a form of idolatry which included such inclinations as trusting in purchasing power in times of trouble rather than trusting in God, expecting to find contentment in material goods rather than seeking

52. Sermon 87 and Sermon 108, I.1–I.8, *Works* 3:228–36, 520–26.

53. Sermon 28, §13, Sermon 80, "On Friendship with the World," §3, Sermon 108, I.1, *Works* 1:620; 3:128–29, 521.

54. Sermon 108, II.2–8, Works 3:524–27.

55. Sermon 68, "The Wisdom of God's Counsels," §16, *Works* 2:561. Similar questions can also be found in Sermon 131, II.10, 11, *Works* 4:183.

happiness in God, living by the standards of the worldly rather than according to God's Moral Law, and making acquisitiveness the ultimate goal of life rather than making present and future salvation the aim.[56]

To the end of his life, Wesley denounced the vice of conspicuous accumulation evident among the Methodists. In 1790, months before his death, Wesley published one last warning to the Methodists contrasting wealthy living and holy living. The reason that more Methodists failed to reach the Altogether stage was not a deficiency in the doctrines preached by the Methodists, he stated, but because they did not follow the threefold resolution to "Gain all you can. Save all you can. Give all you can."[57] Wesley lamented the lack of self-discipline:

> I am distressed. I know not what to do. I see what I might have done once. I might have said peremptorily and expressly: "Here I am: I and my Bible. I will not, I dare not vary from this book, either in great things or small. I have no power to dispense with one jot or tittle of what is contained therein. I am determined to be a Bible Christian, not almost but altogether. Who will meet me on this ground? Join me on this, or not at all." With regard to dress in particular I might have been as firm (and I now see it would have been far better) as either the people called Quakers or the Moravian Brethren. I might have said: "This is *our* manner of dress, which we know is both scriptural and rational. If you join with us you are to dress as we do; but you need not join us unless you please." But alas! The time is now past. And what I can do now I cannot tell.[58]

Years earlier, Wesley had identified doctrinal confusion as the reason why more Methodists did not reach the Altogether stage, and he revised the practice of home visitation to address the lack of vitality evident among his followers. In this sermon he instead wondered if his failure to set a membership requirement that regulated attire had contributed to the decline of holiness among the Methodists.

The general rules to be followed by every member of the Methodist societies did include a resolution to forgo gold jewelry and expensive clothing; however, to be consistent with his usual practice of discipline Wesley should have written not just a resolution but also examination questions to

56. Sermon 28, "Sermon on the Mount, VIII," and Sermon 29, "Sermon on the Mount, IX," §§8–11, *Works* 1:612–31, 636–37; and *Notes* Matt 6:19.

57. Sermon 122, "Causes of the Inefficacy of Christianity," §§8–16, *Works* 4:90–95.

58. Sermon 122, §12, *Works* 4:93.

be asked by class leaders that evaluated members' attempts to stay true to this standard of conduct.

Wesley could have drawn upon the treatise "Advice to the People called Methodists with regard to Dress" (included in the fourth volume of his doctrinal sermons) for resolutions and examination questions related to attire. Neatness and plainness of dress is the standard for apparel that Wesley advised the Methodists to follow. This would have meant resolving to keep their clothing clean, to purchase inexpensive clothes, and to wear modest outfits.[59]

Potentially, the Methodists could have derived daily examination questions such as these from the treatise's argument against costly apparel:

1. Has a single intention to please God prescribed both what clothing I bought, and the manner wherein it was made, and how I put it on and wore it?
2. Have I followed the commands in 1 Timothy 2:9,10 and 1 Peter 3:3,4?
3. Is conformity to worldly standards of outward adornment destroying my conformity to Christ?
4. Did I spend as little as possible on apparel so that I might have more to contribute to the needy?
5. How will this day's purchases be judged on the Last Day?[60]

Christ's final examination figures prominently in an incident involving spending habits and clothing that Wesley recounted from his Oxford days. In his sermon "On Dress," he described seeing a young woman without a decent winter coat. He wanted to help her, but he had little money to give her because he had recently bought decorative pictures for his room. The thought immediately struck him, "Well done, good and faithful steward! Thou hast adorned thy walls with the money which might have screened this poor creature from the cold! O justice! O mercy! Are not these pictures the blood of this poor maid!"[61]

Methodist attire was not the only money-related resolution that Wesley failed to pair with an examination question. He also omitted disciplinary questions regarding the faithful use of money.

59. *SOSO* 4:149.

60. *SOSO* 4:151–54.

61. Sermon 88, §16 *Works* 2:255.

Wesley's Oxford diaries and account book contain records of the money he donated to the poor and the contributions he made to charities. In addition to these monetary gifts, his records show that he also gave away food, medicine, clothing, and books.[62] The Oxford diaries do not, however, contain daily examination questions on his use of money.

Resolutions for managing money appear in many of his publications, but only a few of his sermons include examination questions. His personal resolution was to gain, save, and then give away as much of his money as he could, and he invited his critics to hold him to that standard: "if I leave behind me ten pounds (above my debts and the little arrears of my fellowship) you and all mankind bear witness against me that 'I lived and died a thief and a robber.'" Wesley did not mention how he went about holding himself accountable to this ideal. (After his death, Wesley's biographers made a point of noting that most of his property was bequeathed to the Methodist conference.)[63]

Wesley expected the Methodists to be as thrifty and charitable as he was. He wrote resolutions for the class and band members that directed them to be diligent and frugal and to give alms. For the Altogether, who made up the membership of select societies, a higher standard was set; Wesley's rule for this group required the members to donate as much money as they could to a common fund. These resolutions for Methodist small groups are not paired with any examination questions, however.[64]

Before becoming a preacher, candidates were asked about their level of debt, but no other examination questions related to money are included in the conference *Minutes*, not even in the lists of questions that the preachers were supposed to ask during home visitations. The questions focus on members' faculty of understanding as it related to Methodist doctrine, but very little is asked about the effect that "the desire of the flesh, the desire of the eye, and the pride of life" was having on the affections, will, or liberty.

In contrast to his sermons that condemn worldly desires, Wesley's first sermon on the resolution to gain, save, and give sounds more like his pre-Aldersgate advice. The Methodists were to gain all they could through

62. Heitzenrater, "Oxford Methodists," 70, 71, 122, 139, 142, 390, 402–6.

63. Sermon 87, "The Danger of Riches," II.6, "Earnest Appeal," §96, *Works* 3:237–38; 11:87, 88. Rack, *Reasonable Enthusiast*, 532; and Whitehead, *Life of the Rev. John Wesley*, 553.

64. "General Rules," §5, "Directions given to the Band Societies," II.1, 3, and "A Plain Account of the Methodists," III.3, *Works* 9:72, 79, 270. There is no evidence that the Select Societies kept this resolution, *Works* 10:137, n 153.

honest means without injuring their health, without endangering their lives, and without hurting their souls or their neighbor's substance, body, or soul. They were to be diligent on the job, to strive for quality, and to continually learn about their profession and improve their effectiveness. The Methodists were to save all they could by forgoing idle expenses. They should only purchase the necessities of life (plain food, clothing, and lodging) for themselves and their families. They should bequeath to their heirs an amount sufficient for these basic goods. If the Methodists followed these guidelines, then they would have money left to give to the poor.[65]

Understanding and willpower are all that are needed to follow this resolution. The sermon provides the Methodists with questions that would bolster their resolve. If they ever had doubts about the legitimacy of a purchase, they should examine their attitude (were they thinking like a steward or a proprietor?); they should search Scripture (were they acting in obedience to God's Word?); they should note their intention (were they offering this expense up to God?); and they should consider it in relationship to the Last Judgment (would they be rewarded for this action?).[66]

Once the Methodists understood themselves as merely the stewards of goods entrusted to them by God, exerted their willpower, and followed these prudent financial regulations, then they would be virtuous and generous. Repentance and faith as precursors to holiness (in this case, outward holiness expressed through the righteous use of money) are not mentioned.[67]

Not until the 1780s did Wesley begin to write sermons about riches that included repentance and faith as necessary steps to holiness in respect to this area of Methodist living. These sermons note that resisting the lure of wealth was only possible by grace, and they asked examination questions about Methodist spending habits.[68]

For those who had disposable income and wondered what they should do with it, the Methodists were asked: "Canst thou find none that need the necessaries of life? That are pinched with cold or hunger? None that have not raiment to put on? Or a place where to lay their head? Canst thou find

65. Sermon 50, "The Use of Money," *Works* 2:266–80.

66. Sermon 50, III.4, *Works* 2:278.

67. Sermon 50, §3, I.8, III.7, *Works* 2:268, 273, 279.

68. Sermon 61, §34, Sermon 87, II.2, 9, 20, Sermon 108, II.11, 12, *Works* 2:468; 3:237, 240, 245–46, 528.

none that are wasted with pining sickness? None that are languishing in prison?"[69]

The Methodists were also quizzed on their resolve to gain, save, and give. They were to question their desire to have more than simple food, clothing, and shelter. They were to search their souls to see if they still had the same degree of faith, hope, and love that they had enjoyed before they became rich.[70]

Interestingly, none of Wesley's sermons on money suggests that the questions he posed in them should be part of a daily or weekly review of one's spending habits. In this one area of Christian conduct, Wesley broke with his usual practice of discipline; he did not follow up a specific resolution with a related examination question on which the Methodists were to regularly reflect. In the early years of the revival, Wesley had revised his organization-wide disciplinary system by adding classes, home visits, and doctrinal questions in order to encourage the Methodists to seek the Altogether stage. His concerns about the temptation posed by wealth, however, did not motivate him to further revise Methodist discipline.

Wesley failed to follow his own principle. Without the discipline of individual and corporate examinations, the resolution to gain, save, and give was not protected. Without prudential regulations, this aspect of Wesley's advice was despised and the essence of it lost. Consequently, the spirit of heart religion evaporated, and the Methodists were left with the residue of a once vibrant movement. Their doctrinal clarity, their diligent pursuit of Christ-likeness, and their use of the form of religion could not insulate them from the degenerative influence of excessive wealth.

If Methodism is to be vital, then a revision of Wesley's advice will be necessary.

69. Sermon 126, "On Worldly Folly," I.4, *Works* 4:134.

70. Sermon 87, II.2, 12, Sermon 108, II.10, Sermon 131, *Works* 3:236, 241, 527; 4:186.

FIVE

Designing Methodist Vitality

How then is it possible that Methodism, that is, the religion of the heart, though it flourishes now as a green bay-tree, should continue in this state? For the Methodists in every place grow diligent and frugal; consequently they increase in goods. Hence they proportionably increase in pride, in anger, in the desire of the flesh, the desire of the eyes, and the pride of life. So, although the form of religion remains, the spirit is swiftly vanishing away.

—*Thoughts upon Methodism*

In Wesley's unrelenting critique of wealth-loving Methodists, a faint echo of Paul's advice to Timothy can be heard. Timothy was instructed to exhort the wealthy and tell them they should trust in God's providence rather than in their riches, should be generous, and should be rich in good works (1 Tim 6:17–19). Similarly, Wesley advised the Methodists to place their confidence in God rather than in wealth, to donate to charitable causes generously, and to do all the good they could.

There are differences in the specific recommendations given by Paul and Wesley, however. For example, in terms of fashion, the temptations of Paul's era were not the same as those that enticed the Methodists. Paul instructed Christian women to dress in modest and decent attire, suitable and inexpensive clothes. Wesley expanded on this general guideline and judged that clothing adorned with ruffles was immodest and could not be worn at band meetings. Paul reproved women who braided their hair and embellished it with gold and pearls, while Wesley reacted to the wearing of high-crowned hats as if it were the eighteenth-century equivalent of indecent adornment.[1]

Too many intervening years stood between Paul and Wesley, too many aspects of human culture had changed for Wesley to advise the Methodists by simply quoting the apostle. Some reinterpretation of Paul's instructions, some adjustment for eighteenth-century circumstances was necessary. Likewise, the inheritors of the Wesleyan tradition must engage in a similar process of adaptation in order to make Wesley's advice relevant for current conditions. Wesley's theory of Methodist vitality needs to be translated out of eighteenth-century sensibilities and into those of the twenty-first century.

Translating Wesley

Wesley's theory of Methodist vitality depends on several terms and definitions that are now arcane. His notion of the soul, his definitions of the form and power of religion, his developmental model of salvation, and his concerns about backsliding must all be explained in the vernaculars of today.

The Soul

The concept of an embodied soul implicit in Wesley's writings (i.e., identifying the brain as the bodily organ that the soul primarily uses to carry out its functions) indicates that Wesley was familiar with eighteenth-century medical theories of the body-soul connection. Wesley favored the electrical theory as the most plausible explanation of the relationship between the soul and the body, a theory that conceived of the soul as an electrical fire that moved through the nerves in a manner similar to the way electricity moves through a conductive material.[2]

The incorporation of scientific theories into Wesley's theology, while intriguing, means that Methodists have inherited an eighteenth-century theory of the soul that is incongruent with current psychological theories. Terms such as "faculties of the soul" are no longer in use, and debates about the nature of those faculties, whether or not they include the

1. 1 Tim 2:9; "Large" *Minutes*, 1763, [§18.1] *Works* 10:849; and Wesley to William Church, 13 October 1778, *Letters*.

2. Felleman, "Necessary Relationship," 142–53.

understanding, will, affections, and liberty, have been superseded by other academic arguments.

Wesley's theory of the spiritual senses is also outdated. It reflects a religious epistemology that Wesley came across in 1726 when he read a text by the physician Dr. George Cheyne. That work, *Philosophical Principles of Religion: Natural and Revealed*, assumed that the faculty of understanding depended on sensory information to accurately perform its function, an empirical theory that implied that knowledge of God and the things of God was also sensory dependent. Cheyne theorized that spiritual senses and divine senses allowed one to discern the spiritual realm just as physical senses made it possible to gain insight about the material world.[3]

While neuroscientists and philosophers may disagree over the manner in which human consciousness arises out of unconscious nerve impulses, hormone levels, neural transmitters, blood flow, and neuron connections, they do agree that knowledge depends on more than sensory information—physical or otherwise. Sense data does not flow unimpeded from the sense organs into our awareness. Our abilities to think, reason, and decide can be influenced by unconscious cognitive biases that distort our perception of reality and color our perspective.[4]

Assurance of salvation is another Wesleyan concept that is rooted in an eighteenth-century theory that is no longer current. Certainty, in the eighteenth-century meaning of the term, was viewed as a continuum—the more reliable the evidence, the higher the degree of certainty that an idea, theory, or decision was correct. Wesley adapted this viewpoint and argued that faith provided the most reliable evidence of the divine realm and that those who had faith possessed the highest degree of certainty that their notions of God and the things of God were accurate.[5]

Neuroscientists have discovered that feelings of certitude are not dependent on evidence but instead emerge from activity in the orbitofrontal cortex. A conviction of certainty can be generated even with facts that are questionable and with evidence that is disputed.[6]

These neurological insights into brain functions mean that a revision of the Methodist doctrine of the soul is necessary if the teachings of the church are to be relevant to a scientifically literate audience. Currently, Dr.

3. Felleman, "Evidence of Things Not Seen," 41–64.

4. Lehrer, *How We Decide*; and Marcus, *Kluge*.

5. Felleman, "Degrees of Certainty in Wesley's Natural Philosophy," 59–60.

6. Burton, *On Being Certain*.

William Abraham of Perkins School of Theology is at work on just such a project. He has organized a team of researchers from various disciplines to collaborate on the development of a neuro-theology.[7]

Another resource for those interested in collaborating on the effort to update Methodist doctrinal definitions of the soul is the blog for this book, *Methodist Doctrine, Spirit, Discipline*, which provides a forum where ideas and sources can be exchanged and the implications of current psychological theories can be evaluated with others.[8]

Form and Power Today

Wesley's list of outward forms of religion also needs updating, particularly the identification of the prudential means of grace. He used the term "prudential" for such practices as

- Common Christian Means: rules for avoiding evil, doing good, growing in grace, arts of holy living
- Methodist Means: society, class, band meetings
- Preacher Means: meet with society, leaders, bands, visit the sick and well, instructing in homes, relative duties
- Assistant Means: regulate the societies, bands, and books; hold watchnights, love feasts, and quarterly examinations; send Wesley accounts of preachers' defects
- Fruitful Means: watching against temptations, self-denial, taking up our cross, exercising the presence of God[9]

Wesley observed that spiritual practices could be prudent for a while and then grow less effective over time. His model of ministry recognized that the practice of certain outward forms of religion could grow formal and deadening. Whenever that happened, ineffective exercises would need to be replaced with new forms that successfully conveyed grace and promoted maturation in faith.[10] The United Methodist General Board of Discipleship

7. Abraham, "Brain Battles."
8. Felleman, http://formandpower.blogspot.com/p/forum.html.
9. "Large" *Minutes* (1763), [§40.6–7], *Works* 10:857–58.
10. "Plain Account of the Methodists," II.9, *Works* 9:262–63.

is one resource for those seeking information about current prudential means that others are finding fruitful.

Contemporary versions of Methodist assemblies, such as home visits and class meetings, are needed to ensure that the church's programs are producing vital faith. United Methodist pastors William Easum and Richard Wills have published accounts of their efforts to organize small groups within their congregations. The office of Accountable Discipleship at the General Board of Discipleship is another resource church leaders can utilize when designing such programs for their churches.

A church vitality program should also offer members contemporary models of the Instituted Means of Grace, explained in such a way that they understand what it means to claim that these practices convey God's grace:

- Works of Piety
    - » Prayer
    - » Searching the Scriptures
    - » The Lord's Supper
    - » Fasting
    - » Holy conversations
- Works of Mercy
    - » Giving alms
    - » Providing for the poor
    - » Caring for the sick
    - » Visiting the prisoner[11]

One resource for those seeking a contemporary model for holy conversation is provided by Bob Farr, Director of the Center for Congregational Excellence at the Missouri Annual Conference. "Speaking a Blessing" is part of Reverend Farr's strategy for fostering lay and clergy members' engagement with the nonchurched in their community. By first building relationships with the nonchurched, and then interjecting a faith perspective into their conversations (i.e., offering to pray, sharing beliefs, or describing church involvement), Farr has seen these types of conversation become means of grace that not only bless the nonchurched but that also become practices that build up the faith of church members as well.[12]

11. Sermon 92, II.5, 9; and "Large" *Minutes* (1763), [§40.1–5], *Works* 3:313; 10:855–57; and *Notes* Matt 25:35.

12. Farr, *Renovate or Die*, 79–87, and "Healthy Church Initiative."

The Form and Power of Religion

Defining the power of religion is another design element church leaders must address. Wesley's definition focused on God's grace and the transformational effects of that divine power. Typically, his discussions identified love of God and neighbor as the goal toward which the power moved believers. This phrase was by no means the only scriptural reference he cited in his attempt to explain the goal of religion, as this passage illustrates:

> Look at it again: survey it on every side, and that with the closest attention. In one view, it is purity of intention, dedicating all the life to God. It is the giving God all our heart; it is one desire and design ruling all our tempers. It is the devoting not a part, but all our soul, body, and substance to God. In another view, it is all the mind which was in Christ, enabling us to walk as Christ walked. It is the circumcision of the heart from all filthiness; all inward as well as outward pollution. It is a renewal of the heart in the whole image of God, the full likeness of him that created it. Yet in another, it is the loving God with all our heart, and our neighbour as ourselves. Now take it in which of these views you please, (for there is no material difference,) and this is the whole and sole perfection, as a train of writings prove to a demonstration, which I have believed and taught for these forty years, from the year 1725, to the year 1765.[13]

A church vitality program that reflects Wesley's ministry should articulate the characteristics of those at the highest stage of salvation. Identifying which passages of Scripture and which metaphors most effectively motivate members to pursue that goal will require experimentation and observation. Terminology such as "Christian perfection," "renewal of the *imago Dei*," or "Altogether Christian" may no longer speak to a contemporary audience. Church leaders must discover, as Wesley had to discover, the vocabulary that does inspire Christians to pursue the prize of their high calling (Phil 3:14).

The Developmental Model of Salvation

Preaching and teaching that explained the stages of salvation leading up to the Altogether was another essential element of Wesley's Methodist vitality

13. *Plain Account of Christian Perfection*, §27, *Works* (Jackson) 11:444.

program. His preaching produced fruits by waking people out of spiritual lethargy and sustaining within them a spiritual hunger for righteousness. This was accomplished by telling people that they were caught in a predicament, explaining the nature and consequences of their dire situation, and introducing Christ as the solution for what ailed them.

Wesley's preaching agenda for his assistants required them to preach on each of the developmental stages in the salvation process. Methodist publications taught the Methodists what they could expect to experience as they moved through the various stages from the Asleep to the Altogether. Those expectations helped the Methodists distinguish those who had the power of religion from those who did not.

Today's preachers and teachers must find their own voices and explain salvation in terms that are meaningful and persuasive to their audiences and that encourage Christian maturation. To accurately reflect Wesley's viewpoint, instruction on the way of salvation should retain his emphasis on the necessity of faith in Christ, describe the goal of the Christian life, and teach that this goal is attainable by grace through faith.

Backsliding

Finally, a Church vitality program in the Wesleyan tradition will include an explanation of the obstacles that will hinder advancement towards that goal. Wesley identified the common causes of backsliding, and he advised his followers on the best ways to guard against those pernicious influences, especially the temptation posed by increasing wealth.

Materialism continues to be a temptation, although other modern issues (resentment of immigrants, suspicion of other races, unsustainable consumption, etc.) should not be ignored. These social tensions also inhibit progress towards the goal of the Christian life and contribute to backsliding. Church leaders should be observant, notice what interferes with congregants' growth in grace, and advise them accordingly.

Design Elements

An effective plan for church revitalization modeled after Wesley's ministry should include certain elements that are distinctive to Methodism and that reflect the insights that our leader acquired as he learned by experience.

A Balanced Design

As church leaders design their Methodist vitality programs, they would do well to keep the same balance that Wesley maintained between the various components of his design. After his Aldersgate experience, Wesley was always careful to explain the relationship between the form and power of religion in such a way that one did not overshadow the other. Divine grace is always distinguished as the initiator and sustainer of a process to which humans prudently respond.[14]

His metaphors of spiritual respiration and spiritual re-action are examples of his attempt to maintain the correct balance between divine-human interaction. He portrayed spiritual respiration as a cycle that begins when God descends into the regenerated and breaths the power of religion into them. Their spiritual senses open up in re-action to this power, and these newly awakened senses help them choose between good and evil and discern God's activity in their lives. The more the spiritual senses are used, the more they are strengthened, which increases both Christians' love for God and their understanding of the things of God. In reply to God's grace, believers breathe out forms of religion such as prayers and praise that ascend to God. The cycle begins anew when God's power redescends upon the faithful in response to their prayers.[15]

Besides Wesley's balanced treatment of the form and power of religion, he also balanced the roles played by doctrine, spirit, and discipline in his ministry plan. Doctrine balances spirit and discipline by making faith in Christ the foundation for outward practices and inward experiences, and by identifying grace as the power that facilitates progress through the stages of salvation. Without these doctrinal standards, Wesley's system would have degenerated into works righteousness.

He used his own story to illustrate the enervating effects of following the wrong order of salvation. The Oxford Methodists searched for heart religion—"a religion of love, and joy, and peace, having its seat in the inmost soul, but ever showing itself by its fruits, continually springing forth, not only in all innocence, (for love worketh no ill to his neighbour,) but likewise in every kind of beneficence, spreading virtue and happiness all around it"—by adhering to the instructions offered in religious advice

14. Maddox, *Responsible Grace.*

15. Sermon 19, II.1, III.2, 3, and Sermon 45, II.4, *Works* 1: 435–36, 442; 2:193.

books.[16] This advice, "the reading, fasting, praying, denying ourselves,—the going to church, and to the Lord's table,—the relieving the poor, visiting those that were sick and in prison, instructing the ignorant, and labouring to reclaim the wicked," did not give them the experience of the power of religion and the renewal of the *imago Dei* that they sought, but rather left Wesley and his university friends feeling listless and weary ("both of the world and of ourselves").[17]

In order to spare others this same sense of futility and frustration, Wesley shared what his experience had taught him: that heart religion was a gift given by grace through faith. Only repentance then faith then holiness would lead to love of God and neighbor. All other doctrinal orders were vain and fruitless.[18]

Methodist Doctrine also recognizes that Christians will be at different faith stages and that each stage will need its own form of discipline if growth in grace is to be nurtured. Wesley's doctrinal teachings guarded against disciplinary standards that could potentially demoralize new converts who did not immediately sense the power of God's love. His teachings also discouraged lax discipline that allowed Methodists to cease expecting the Altogether stage and consequently to devolve into spiritually complacent, self-satisfied backsliders.

The Methodist spirit balances doctrine and discipline by providing a goal for the Christian life and a standard of evaluation. Doctrinal teachings and disciplinary practices are judged according to the ideal of holiness, happiness, and certainty. Wesley's career-long criticism of the doctrine of predestination is one example of the way he used the Methodist spirit to determine which doctrines could be taught in his preaching houses and which could not. In multiple publications, Wesley reported his observation that belief in predestination hindered an individual's pursuit of inward and outward holiness and undermined happiness and certainty. This was one of the reasons Wesley prohibited the discussion of predestination at Methodist society meetings.[19]

16. "Earnest Appeal," §4, *Works* 11:46.

17. "Earnest Appeal," §§8, 71, *Works* 11:47, 75.

18. "Earnest Appeal," §5, *Works* 11:46.

19. Sermon 20, "The Lord Our Righteousness," II.19, Sermon 35, "The Law Established through Faith, I," and Sermon 110, "Free Grace," Journal entry, 19 June 1740, *Works* 1:462; 2:20–32; 3:544–63; 19:152–53; "A Dialogue between an Antinomian and his friend," and "A Blow at the Root," §8, *Works* (Jackson) 10:276, 366.

The insistence that both inward and outward holiness are essential elements of the Methodist spirit meant that works of mercy were deemed just as important to Methodist discipline as works of piety. Good works such as "feeding the hungry, clothing the naked, entertaining the stranger, visiting those that are in prison, or sick, or variously afflicted . . . endeavoring to instruct the ignorant, to awaken the stupid sinner, to quicken the lukewarm, to confirm the wavering, to comfort the feebleminded, to succour the tempted" were as important as prayer, fasting, and other works of piety. Methodists were encouraged to practice both forms while waiting for the power of religion.[20]

Discipline balances doctrine and spirit by joining heaven and earth. Discipline ensures that human conceptions of religion do not replace divine expectations. By making the Last Judgment the model for Methodist evaluation, discipline keeps Methodism heavenly minded instead of worldly worried. To be judged a faithful steward of Christ, not a pleaser of people or a servant of human institutions, becomes the measure of faithfulness. Because of this perspective on ministry, Wesley continued to teach his order of salvation, to preach throughout the British Isles, and to employ lay preachers even when other priests of the Church of England objected to these practices and incited mob violence against the Methodists.

By pairing a resolution with an examination question, discipline ensured that teachings about the order of salvation and the goal of the Christian life were more than intellectual understandings but were personally appropriated by Methodists until they made the pursuit of the Altogether stage a lifelong habit.

The Marks of Effectiveness

Once a church vitality program is up and running, leaders will want to monitor its effectiveness and ensure that it is in fact helping people become better, more faithful Christians. To do that, church leaders must decide on the measurements that will be used as evidence of spiritual growth. Wesley used the characteristics of holiness, happiness, and certainty to identify who was progressing towards the Altogether stage. Ministry effectiveness was measured by the number of people who repented, experienced faith, and whose lives went on to reflect love for God and neighbor (even enemies),

20. Sermon 43, "The Scripture Way of Salvation," III.9, 10, *Works* 2:166.

zeal for good works, and happiness in all circumstances.[21] Resolutions to seek this goal were always paired with examination questions that encouraged self-reflection and group accountability.

Some comparable measurements and examinations must be used to evaluate the dispositions and habitual inclinations of those who participate in Church vitality programs. Indicators that simply track outward forms, such as attendance and donations, do not adequately reflect the Wesleyan commitment to heart religion.

Training Effective Leaders

Designing a plan for ministry that woke people out of their spiritual complacency and awoke within them a longing for God's grace was a challenging task for Wesley. The years that transpired between his ordination and his Aldersgate experience were filled with moments of personal and professional frustration.

Even after he understood that the experience he wanted would only come through faith in Christ and had made that faith the foundation of his religious practices, Wesley still found it difficult to persuade others to follow his teachings. He struggled to keep the Methodists moving towards the Altogether stage, and he was convinced that many of them were not as vital as they should have been. That someone with Wesley's intellectual and organizational skills struggled to become an effective minister should give all of us who follow him reason to pause.

Part of what inhibited Wesley's ministry was the education he received. His studies in Aristotelian moral philosophy had not given him the theological understanding he needed in order to preach effective sermons. After he revised his conception of the doctrine of justification by faith he had a greater impact on people and reported more success at influencing the lives of others for the better.

Wesley's experience reveals the potential inadequacies of theological education. Not every theology is conducive to pastoral ministry. Discovering which ones will guide congregants through the developmental stages of salvation and which will not is a time-consuming task. Thirteen years passed before Wesley finally clarified his understanding of the human condition, the goal of religion, and the supports and obstacles to growth in

21. Sermon 18, "The Marks of the New Birth," *Works* 1:417–30.

grace. Most ordination boards are not going to wait that long for pastors to figure out how to implement a Church vitality program. Denominational officials seek pastoral leaders who can have an immediate and fruitful impact upon a congregation. Seminaries could help train such leaders by including field-based assignments in every Master of Divinity course.

Such an educational model would be more consistent with current neurological theories than the present classroom-based curriculum. Researchers have found that the brain learns new skills through a process of trial and error. By experimenting in real-life situations and experiencing success and failure, students practice and hone professional skills.[22]

Pedagogy that combines thinking and feeling is the most effective way to teach students. People learn as much from positive feedback as from negative if they have a mentor who can explain what went wrong with an experiment, the flaws in its design, and how those mistakes can inform a new strategy. This is the model of professional education that Donald Schön described in his study of professional schools. Whether the institution was a school of business, law, medicine, architecture, engineering, psychology, or music, every successful educational program for professionals included a supervised design laboratory where students worked with the materials of their profession and fashioned a solution to a professional challenge under the guidance of an experienced mentor.[23]

In the case of seminary education, the professional challenge that seminary students must respond to is the tendency for ministries to lose the form and the power of religion. To design a model of ministry that resists that trend will require different types of professional skills including exegetical, theological, homiletical, sociological, psychological, pedagogical, and liturgical. To become proficient at these skills, students must put them to use, apply them in real-life ministry situations, and receive critical feedback on their efforts.

In order to offer these types of learning laboratories, a revision of the Master of Divinity curriculum will be necessary. Currently, seminaries offer at most two opportunities for supervised ministry. More opportunities for designing, testing, and mentoring are needed to help students develop the skills needed to implement a plan for Church vitality similar to the one designed by Wesley.

22. Schwartz and Sharpe, *Practical Wisdom*.

23. Schön, *The Reflective Practitioner*; and Schön, *Educating the Reflective Practitioner*.

A Redesign Checklist

In 2008 the General Conference of The United Methodist Church voted to revise the denomination's mission statement. After the phrase "to make disciples of Jesus Christ," the clause "for the transformation of the world" was added. Creating an effective disciple-making plan that produced church members who went out and transformed the world was a task left to the imagination and ingenuity of individual church leaders.

John Wesley had a plan for making disciples that viewed transformation, whether individual or global, as a work of grace. Disciple-making depended upon this divine power; however, it also required individual and corporate spiritual disciplines. The Methodists were vital as long as they maintained a balance between grace and works by holding fast to Wesley's order of salvation, his definition of the goal of the Christian life, and his practice of resolving and examining.

Instead of a generic program that could be adopted by any Protestant denomination, I have provided the checklist below to illustrate the steps church leaders should take when designing and implementing a distinctively Methodist vitality program for their congregations. In order for their program to be consistent with Wesley's ministry, the following tasks should be accomplished:

1. Translate Wesley's definitions
    a. Human predicament
    b. Salvation by faith
    c. Holiness of heart and life, happiness, and certainty
    d. Divine initiative and human prudence
    e. Stages of salvation
    f. Present and future salvation
    g. Causes of backsliding

2. Update Wesley's methods
    a. Means of grace
    b. Resolutions and examinations

3. Balanced Design
    a. Offer forms of religion that point participants to the power of religion
    b. Offer forms of religion for each stage of salvation

   c. Educate participants on Methodist doctrine, spirit, and discipline
   d. Provide opportunities to engage in both works of piety and works of mercy

4. Evaluate Results
   a. Do participants understand the program's revised Wesleyan terminology?
   b. Does the program motivate and inspire participants to become better, more faithful Christians?
5. Revise Program
   a. Clarify definitions of Wesleyan terms
   b. Test different means of grace
   c. Try different resolution and examination methods

Wesley's legacy is an approach to ministry that supports both the form and the power of religion, and honoring that legacy requires effort and skill. Carrying out Wesley's advice to preserve Methodist doctrine, spirit, and discipline will not be easy. Resisting the influences that would turn a church into a dead sect is a constant challenge, and identifying the means that will transform a church into a vital congregation requires continual experimentation.

You are a minister. You know that performing these tasks is beyond your talent and ability. It will require a power greater than your own to accomplish this mission. Thanks be to God that such a power exists.

Bibliography

Abraham, William J. "Brain Battles: Theology, Neuroscience, and the Search for the Soul." Paper presented at Ministers Week, Perkins School of Theology, Dallas, TX, 3 February 2010.

Allestree, Richard. *The Causes of the Decay of Christian Piety*. London: R. Norton, 1667.

———. *The Whole Duty of Man*. London: Printed for T. Garthwait, 1659.

Asbury, Francis. *The Heart of Asbury's Journal*. Edited by Ezra Squire Tipple. New York: Eaton & Mains, 1904.

Austin, John. *Devotions in the Ancient Way of Offices*. Edited by William Birchley. London: George Hickes, 1701.

Bill, E. G. W. *Education at Christ Church, Oxford, 1660–1800*. Oxford: Clarendon, 1988.

Burton, Robert A. *On Being Certain: Believing Your Are Right Even When You're Not*. New York: St. Martin's, 2008.

Burton-Edwards, Taylor. "Commentary: A Missional Future—The United Methodist Way." *UM Portal* (March 24, 2008). No pages. Online: www.umportal.org/article.asp?id=3283.

Campbell, Ted. *John Wesley and Christian Antiquity: Religious Vision and Cultural Change*. Nashville: Kingswood, 1991.

Cape, Kim. "Petition 20173—Complaint Process Revision: Administrative Location." No Pages. Online: http://calms.umc.org/2012/Menu.aspx?type=Petition&mode=Single&number=173.

Coyner, Michael J. "857 Plus One, Two, Three, Four, Five, and Seven." An E-pistle from Bishop Mike (November 12, 2007). No pages. Online: www.inumc.org/epistles/detail/43266.

DeShon, Richard P., and Abigail Quinn. *Job Analysis Generalizability Study for the Position of United Methodist Local Pastor: Focus Group Results*. Michigan State University, 15 December 2007. Online: www.gbhem.org/atf/cf/%7B0bcef929-bdba-4aa0-968f-d1986a8eef80%7D/bom_jobanalysisdeshon.pdf.

Eisenstein, Elizabeth L. *The Printing Press as an Agent of Change: Communications and Cultural Transformations in Early Modern Europe*. 2 vols. Cambridge: Cambridge University Press, 1979.

Elmen, Paul. "Richard Allestree and *The Whole Duty of Man*." *The Library* 5 (1951) 19–27.

English, John C. "John Wesley's Studies as an Undergraduate." *Proceedings of the Wesley Historical Society* 47 (May 1989) 29–37.

Eustache de Saint-Paul. "A Compendium of Philosophy in Four Parts [*Summa philosophiae quadripartita*, 1609]." In *Descartes' Meditations: Background Source Materials*, edited by Roger Ariew, John Cottingham, and Tom Sorell, 68–96. Cambridge: Cambridge University Press, 1998.

———. *Ethica, sive, Summa moralis disciplinae in tres partes divisa*. London: J. Redmayne, 1677.

Farr, Bob. "Healthy Church Initiative." Workshop presented at St. Andrew's United Methodist Church, Omaha, NE, 6 September 2011.

———. *Renovate or Die: Ten Ways to Focus Your Church on Mission*. Nashville: Abingdon, 2011.

Felleman, Laura Bartels. "Degrees of Certainty in John Wesley's Natural Philosophy." In *Divine Grace and Emerging Creation: Wesleyan Forays in Science and Theology of Creation*, edited by Thomas Jay Oord, 58–80. Eugene, OR: Wipf & Stock, 2009.

———. "The Evidence of Things Not Seen: John Wesley's Use of Natural Philosophy." PhD diss., Drew University, 2004.

———. "Forum" *Methodist Doctrine, Spirit, Discipline*. Last modified 14 August 2011. Online: http://formandpower.blogspot.com/p/forum.html.

———. "A Necessary Relationship: John Wesley and the Body-Soul Connection." In *"Inward and Outward Health": John Wesley's Holistic Concept of Medical Science, the Environment, and Holy Living*, edited by Deborah Madden, 140–68. London: Epworth, 2008.

Fiering, Norman S. *Moral Philosophy at Seventeenth-Century Harvard: A Discipline in Transitioin*. Chapel Hill: University of North Carolina Press, 1981.

Fowler, C. F. *Descartes on the Human Soul: Philosophy and the Demands of Christian Doctrine*. Dordrecht: Kluwer Academic, 1999.

Green, Linda. "Convocation Focuses on 'the United Methodist Way.'" News—across the Church. No pages. Online: www.umc.org/site/apps/nl/content3.asp?c=lwL4KnN1LtH&b=2072525&ct=4644277.

Greenwaldt, Karen, Ernest S. Lyght, and Jerome King Del Pino. "Petition 80251—Guaranteed Appointments." No pages. Online: http://calms.umc.org/2008/Menu.aspx?type=Petition&mode=Single&number=251.

Haller, Laurie. "Commentary: Join the Journey on the United Methodist Way." *UM Portal* (January 16, 2008). No pages. Online: www.umportal.org/article.asp?id=2999.

Hammond, Geordan. "Restoring Primitive Christianity: John Wesley and Georgia, 1735–1737." PhD diss., University of Manchester, 2008.

Hammond, Henry. *A practicall catechisme*. Oxford, 1645.

———. *A practicall catechisme*. 5th ed. London: R. Royston, 1649.

Harper, Elizabeth. *An Extract from the Journal of Elizabeth Harper*. Edited by John Wesley. Bristol: W. Pine, 1769.

Heitzenrater, Richard P. "John Wesley and the Oxford Methodists, 1725–1735." PhD diss., Duke University, 1972.

———. *Wesley and the People Called Methodists*. Nashville: Abingdon, 1995.

Henry, Matthew. *An Exposition of All the Books of the Old and New Testament*. Vol. 6. London, 1721–1725.

Ingham, Benjamin. *Diary of an Oxford Methodist, Benjamin Ingham, 1733–1734*. Edited by Richard P. Heitzenrater. Durham: Duke University Press, 1985.

Jackson, Thomas. *The Life of the Rev. Charles Wesley*. Vol. 2. London: Wesleyan Conference Office, 1841.

Kisker, Scott. "Anthony Horneck (1641–1697) and the Rise of Anglican Pietism." PhD diss., Drew University, 2003.

Law, William. *A Practical Treatise upon Christian Perfection*. London: William & John Innys, 1726.

———. *A Serious Call to a Devout and Holy Life*. London: William Innys, 1729.

Lehrer, Jonah. *How We Decide*. Boston: Houghton Mifflin Harcourt, 2009.

Lettinga, Neil. "Covenant Theology Turned Upside Down: Henry Hammond and Caroline Anglican Moralism: 1643–1660." *The Sixteenth Century Journal* 24:3 (1993) 653–69.

Lloyd, Gareth. *Charles Wesley and the Struggle for Methodist Identity*. Oxford: Oxford University Press, 2007.

Maddox, Randy L. "Living the United Methodist Way: Deep Convictions and Cultural Resistance." Paper presented at the Southeastern Jurisdictional Conference, Lake Junaluska, NC, 16 July 2008. Online: http://methodistthinker.com/2010/08/25/podcast-randy-maddox-methodist-doctrine-spirit-discipline/.

———. *Responsible Grace: John Wesley's Practical Theology*. Nashville: Kingswood, 1994.

———. "Wesley's Prescription for Making Disciples of Jesus Christ: Insights for the Twenty-First Century Church." No pages. Online: http://divinity.duke.edu/sites/default/files/documents/faculty-maddox/22_Wesleys_Prescription_Duke.pdf.

Marcus, Gary F. *Kluge: The Haphazard Construction of the Human Mind*. Boston: Houghton Mifflin, 2008.

Marks, Carol L. Introduction to *Christian Ethics*, edited by Thomas Traherne. Ithaca: Cornell University Press, 1968.

Matthews, Rex D. "'Religion and Reason Joined': A Study in the Theology of John Wesley." ThD diss., Harvard University, 1986.

McGiffert, Michael. "Henry Hammond and Covenant Theology." *Church History: Studies in Christianity and Culture* 74:2 (2005) 255–85.

McIntosh, Lawrence. "The Nature and Design of Christianity in John Wesley's Early Theology." PhD diss., Drew University, 1966.

Nelson, Robert. *The Practice of True Devotion*. London: Joseph Downing, 1721.

Norris, John. *A Practical Treatise concerning Humility*. London: S. Manship, 1707.

Overton, John Henry. *John Wesley*. London: Methuen, 1891.

Packer, John William. *The Transformation of Anglicanism, 1643–1660, with Special Reference to Henry Hammond*. Manchester: Manchester University Press, 1969.

Pawson, John. *A Short Account of Mr. John Pawson, in a Letter to the Rev. Mr. John Wesley*. London: R. Hawes, 1779.

Pearson, John. *An Exposition of the Creed*. London: printed for B. Griffin, & Sam. Keble, 1701.

Pinkston, Jeanette, and Erik Alsgaard. "United Methodists Join Forces to 'Turn Worlds Upside Down.'" Living the United Methodist Way: Turning Worlds Upside Down (February 5, 2009). No pages. Online: www.umcquadtraining.org/default.html.

Purcell, Mark. "'Useful Weapons for the Defence of That Cause': Richard Allestree, John Fell and the Foundation of the Allestree Library." *The Library* 6:2 (1999) 124–47.

Rack, Henry D. *Reasonable Enthusiast: John Wesley and the Rise of Methodism*. 3rd ed. London: Epworth, 2002.

Routley, Erik. "Charles Wesley and Matthew Henry." *Congregational Quarterly* 33 (1955) 345–51.

Schön, Donald A. *Educating the Reflective Practitioner*. San Francisco: Jossey-Bass, 1987.

———. *The Reflective Practitioner: How Professionals Think in Action*. New York: Basic Books, 1983.

Schwartz, Barry, and Kenneth Sharpe. *Practical Wisdom: The Right Way to Do the Right Thing*. New York: Riverhead, 2010.

Scougal, Henry. *The Life of God in the Soul of Man*. London: Charles Smith & William Jacob, 1677.

Sharpe, James A. "Social Control in Early Modern England: The Need for a Broad Perspective." In *Social Control in Europe: 1500–1800*, edited by Herman Roodenburg and Pieter Spierenburg, 1:37–54. Columbus: Ohio State University Press, 2004.

Sutherland, L. S., and L. G. Mitchell, editors. *The History of the University of Oxford*. Vol. 5. *The Eighteenth Century*. Oxford: Clarendon, 1986.

Tailfer, Patrick. *A True and Historical Narrative of the Colony of Georgia*. Charlestown, SC: P. Timothy, 1741.

Taylor, Jeremy. *The Rule and Exercises of Holy Living*. London: R. Norton, 1650.

Tennant, R. C. "Christopher Smart and *The Whole Duty of Man*." *Eighteenth-Century Studies* 13 (1979) 63–78.

Thomas à Kempis. *The Christian's Pattern; or, A Divine Treatise of the Imitation of Christ*. Translated by John Worthington. London: R. Daniel, 1657.

Towner, Philip H. *The Letters to Timothy and Titus*. Grand Rapids: Eerdmans, 2006.

Tyerman, Luke. *The Life and Times of the Rev. John Wesley, Founder of the Methodists*. Vol. 3. London: Hodder & Stoughton, 1876.

Tyson, John R. *Assist Me to Proclaim: The Life and Hymns of Charles Wesley*. Grand Rapids: Eerdmans, 2007.

"The United Methodist Way: Living the Christian Life in Covenant with Christ and One Another." No pages. Online: www.gbod.org/site/apps/nlnet/content3.aspx?c=nhLRJ2PMKsG&b=5503325&ct=8540803.

Village United Methodist Church. "Upcoming Events." *The Chimes* (February 2010). No pages. Online: http://www.villageumc.org/The_Chimes/Feb2010.pdf.

Wesley, Charles. *Journal*. Vol. 2. Edited by Thomas Jackson. London: John Mason, 1849.

Wesley, John. *Explanatory Notes upon the New Testament*. Wesley Center Online. http://wesley.nnu.edu/john-wesley/john-wesleys-notes-on-the-bible/.

———. *The Letters of John Wesley*. Edited by John Telford. Wesley Center Online. http://wesley.nnu.edu/john-wesley/the-letters-of-john-wesley/.

———. *Sermons on Several Occassions*. Vol. 4. Bristol: John Grabham, 1760.

———. *The Works of John Wesley. Begun as The Oxford Edition of the Works of John Wesley (Oxford: Clarendon, 1975–83); continued as The Bicentennial Edition of the Works of John Wesley.* General editors, Frank Baker and Richard P. Heitzenrater. Nashville: Abingdon, 1984.

———. *The Works of John Wesley*. Edited by Thomas Jackson. 3rd ed. 1872. Reprint, Grand Rapids: Baker, 2002.

Wesley, John, editor. *Arminian Magazine*. London, 1778–1791.

———. *A Christian Library*. Bristol: Felix Farley, 1749–1755.

Whitaker, Timothy W. "Living the United Methodist Way: An e-Review Commentary." e-Review Florida United Methodist News Service (February 7, 2008). No pages. Online: www.flumc.info/cgi-script/csArticles/articles/000044/004413-p.htm.

Whitehead, John. *The Life of the Rev. John Wesley*. Auburn and Buffalo: John E. Beardsley, 1793.

Index